Keith Johnson

Top Physics Grades for You

GCSE Revision Guide for AQA

Nelson Thornes

Contents

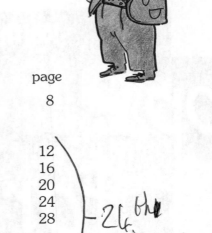

Introduction

Revision Technique

Exam Technique

To see the latest Exam Specification for AQA Science and AQA Physics, visit **www.aqa.org.uk**

To see this Exam Specification 'mapped' with the relevant pages in **Physics for You**, visit **www.physicsforyou.co.uk**

Introduction

Top Physics Grades for You is designed to help you achieve the best possible grades in your GCSE examination.

It focusses on exactly what you need to do to succeed in the AQA Science examinations, whether for Core Science, for Additional Science, or for the full GCSE Physics qualification, and for both Foundation Tier and Higher Tier.

It includes a section on 'How Science works', which is an important part of all the AQA Science examinations.

This revision book is best used together with the ***Physics for You*** textbook, but it can also be used by itself.

There are also books for ***Top Biology Grades for You*** and ***Top Chemistry Grades for You***.

For each section in the AQA GCSE Science examination specification, there is a Topic as shown on the opposite page.

For each Topic there are 2 double-page spreads:

- a **Revision** spread, which shows you exactly what you need to know (see below), and

- a **Questions** spread, which lets you try out Homework questions and some real Exam questions on this topic.
The **Answers** for these, with Examiners' Tips, are given at the back of the book.

In addition, for a section of Topics there is:

- a **Sample Answer** spread, showing you answers at Grade-A level and at Grade-C level, with Examiners' Comments and Tips. These will help you to focus on how to improve, to move up to a higher grade.

Each Revision spread is laid out clearly, using boxes:

Each spread starts with some 'ThinkAbout' questions, to help you focus on the topic. The answers are shown at the bottom of the page.

Topic number and AQA reference

The pages show essential content for the exam.

Items are often boxed for clarity.

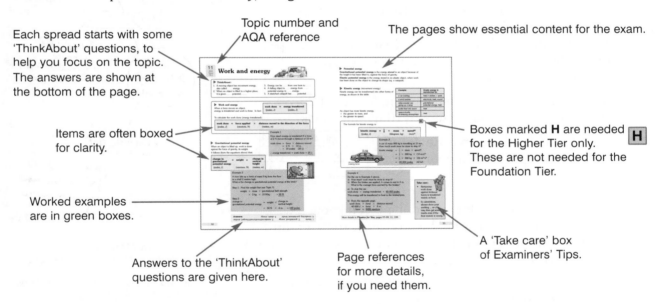

Boxes marked **H** are needed for the Higher Tier only. These are not needed for the Foundation Tier.

Worked examples are in green boxes.

Answers to the 'ThinkAbout' questions are given here.

Page references for more details, if you need them.

A 'Take care' box of Examiners' Tips.

As a first step, go through this book and:

- If you are **not** studying for the Higher Tier, cross out all the boxes labelled **H**

- If you are **not** studying for the full GCSE Physics, cross out all of Topics 18–25.

On the front and back covers of this book there are detachable **Revision Cards,** with very brief summaries.

You can cut these out and use them to top up your revision in spare moments – for example, when sitting on a bus or waiting for a lesson.

Best wishes for a great result in your exams,

Keith Johnson

Revision Technique

Prepare

1. Go through the book, crossing out any boxes that you don't need (as described at the bottom of page 3).

2. While doing this, you can decide which are your strong topics, and which are topics that you need to spend more time on.

3. You need to balance your time between:
   - **Revising** what you need to know about Physics.
     To do this, use the first double-page spread in each topic.
   - **Practising** by doing exam questions.
     To do this, use the second spread in each topic.

   Do these two things for each topic in turn.

Revise

4. Think about your best ways of revising. Some of the best ways are to do something *active*. To use active learning you can:
   - Write down **notes**, as a summary of the topic (while reading through the double-page spread).
     Use highlighter pens to colour key words.
   - Make a **poster** to summarise each topic (and perhaps pin it up on your bedroom wall).
     Make it colourful, and use images/sketches if you can.
   - Make a spider-diagram or **mind map** of each topic.
     See the example here, but use your own style:
   - Ask someone (family or friend) to **test** you on the topic.
   - **Teach** the topic to someone (family or friend).

   Which method works best for you?

5. It is usually best to work in a quiet room, for about 25–30 minutes at a time, and then take a 5–10 minute break.

6. It is often helpful to draw up a **Revision Calendar**, to keep a note of your progress:

Topic 4 AQA 1a.3
✓ 3rd April

Practise

7. When you have revised a topic, and think you know it well, then it's important to practise it, by answering some **exam questions**. Turn to the second spread of the topic and answer the questions as well as you can.

8. When you have finished them, turn to the **Examination answers and tips** that start on page 112.
   Check your answers, and read the Examiner's Tips.
   Can you see how to improve your answers in future?

9. If you have a **Revision Calendar** keep a record of your progress on it.

Topic 4 AQA 1a.3
✓ 3rd April
✓ 4th April

Re-revise and Top-up

10. It is important to re-revise each topic again, after an interval.
    The best intervals are after 10 minutes, after 1 day, and after 1 week (see the graphs in *Physics for You*, pages 382–383).

    For this top-up you can use the topic spread, your notes, poster or mind map, and the **Revision Cards** on the cover of this book.

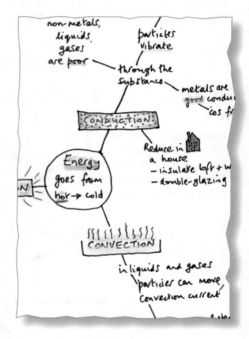

*Part of a **Mind Map** for Topic 2: Conduction, Convection, Radiation.*

*A Mind Map always makes more sense when you make it **yourself**.*

Use colour and images if you can.

A revision flowchart:

Choose a topic to revise.

1. Revise

- **ThinkAbout** : try the questions in the ThinkAbout box.
  The answers are at the bottom of the page.

- **Read** the rest of the double-page spread.
  Focus on any parts you are not sure about.

- **Do** make Notes, or a Poster, or a Mind Map.
  Highlight key points in colour.

- **Re-read** the spread after a break of 5–10 minutes.

- **Take care** : read the 'Take care' box.
  Can you see how you can use this advice?

2. Practise

- **Try** the questions on the double-page of questions.
  These are in the same style as the ones in the exam.

- **Check** your answers. The answers begin on page 112.
  Read the Examiners' Hints carefully.
  Go back over anything you find difficult.

Then later:

Re-visit
Re-visit each topic 1 day later, and then 1 week later.
Read the double-page spread, your notes or Mind Map,
and the questions you answered.

Up your Grade
At the end of each section of topics, read the Sample
Answers at Grade A and Grade C.
Look at the Hints and Tips for improving your grade.

Top-up
Use the Revision Cards to remind you of the key points,
and test yourself.
Even better, make your own Revision Cards.

Examination Technique

Before the exam

1. Make sure you know the dates and times of all your exams, so that you are not late!
   See the table at the bottom of this page.

2. Make sure you know which topics are going to be examined on which paper.

3. On the night before the exam, it may help to do some quick revision – but don't do too much.
   Make sure you get a good night's sleep.

On the day of the exam

1. Aim to arrive early at the exam room.

2. Make sure that you are properly equipped with pens and pencils (including spares), an eraser, a ruler, a calculator (check the battery!) and a watch.

During the exam

1. Don't waste time when you get the paper. Write your name and candidate number (unless they are already printed).
   Read the instructions on the front page of the booklet, carefully, and make sure you follow them.

2. Read each question very carefully.
   In each question there is always a 'command' word that tells you what to do.
   If the question says '*State ...*' or '*List ...*' or '*Name ...*' then you should give a short answer.
   If the question says '*Explain ...*' or '*Describe ...*' or '*Why does ...*' or '*Suggest ...*' then you should make sure you give a longer answer.

   Put a ring round each 'command' word.

   Then underline the key words in the question.
   For example:

   Then you can see exactly what is given to you in the question, and what you have to do.

   Make sure that you answer only the question shown on the exam paper (not the one that you wish had been asked).

Calculate the potential difference across a 5 Ω resistor when a current of 2 A is passing.

Here is one way of collecting information about all your exams (in all your subjects):

Date, time and room	Subject, paper number and tier	Length (time)	Types of question: – structured? – single word answers? – longer answers? – essays?	Sections?	Details of choice (if any)	Approximate time per mark (minutes)
5th June 9.30 Hall	Science Paper 3 (Physics) Higher Tier	45 mins	Structured questions (with single-word answers and longer answers)	1	no choice	1 min.

Answering the questions

Structured questions

- Make sure you know exactly what the question is asking.

- Look for the number of marks awarded for each part of the question. For example *(2 marks)* means that the Examiner will expect 2 main (and different) points in your answer.

- The number of lines of space is also a guide to how much you are expected to write.

- Make sure that you use any data provided in the question.

- Pace yourself with a watch so that you don't run out of time. You should aim to use about 1 minute for each mark. So if a question has 3 marks it should take you about 3 minutes.

- In calculations, show all the steps in your working.
This way you may get marks for the way you tackle the problem, even if your final answer is wrong.
Make sure that you put the correct units on the answer.

- Try to write something for each part of every question.

- Follow the instructions given in the question. If it asks for one answer, give only one answer.

- If you have spare time at the end, use it wisely.

Extended questions

- Some questions require longer answers, where you will need to write two or more full sentences.

- The questions may include the words '***Describe***...' or '***Explain***...' or '***Evaluate***...' or '***Suggest***...' or '***Why does***...'.

- Make sure that the sentences are in good English and are linked to each other.

- Make sure you use scientific words in your answer.

- As before, the marks and the number of lines will give you a guide to how much to write. Make sure you include enough detail with at least as many points as there are marks.

- For the highest grades you need to include full details, in scientific language, written in good English, and with the sentences linking together in the correct sequence.

For multiple-choice questions:
- Read the instructions carefully.
- Mark the answer sheet exactly as you are instructed.
- If you have to rub out an answer, make sure that you rub it out well, so no pencil mark is left.
- Even if the answer looks obvious, look at all the alternatives before making a decision.
- If you are not sure of the answer, then first delete any answers that look wrong.
- If you still don't know the answer, then make an educated guess!
- Ensure that you give an answer to every question.

How Science works

> **ThinkAbout:**
>
> 1. Before starting an investigation, you need to . . . . it, to try to make it a . . . . test.
> 2. Then you can collect . . . ., by . . . . and measuring. You should record your results in a . . . . and then use them to draw a . . . .
> 3. On a line-graph you should try to draw a line of . . . . fit. From the pattern of the graph you should try to draw a . . . .
> 4. Afterwards you should always . . . . the investigation to try to improve it.

The ideas of 'How Science works' are important throughout the course and in the exam papers, but particularly in your ISAs (Investigative Skills Assignments).
Make sure that you understand all the words in **bold**.

> **Collecting evidence**

Your evidence needs to be both *reliable* and *valid*.

Reliable evidence is data we can trust. If someone else did the same experiment, they would get the same result. It would be **reproducible**.
To make your data more reliable, repeat your readings and calculate the mean (average).

Valid evidence is data that is reliable *and* that is relevant to the question being investigated.

> **Taking measurements**

You need to take a **range** of readings that are *accurate* and *precise*.

Accuracy: an expensive thermometer will usually be more accurate than a cheap one. It will give a reading nearer to the *true* temperature.

Precision: a precise instrument will have smaller scale divisions, and will give the same reading again and again under the same conditions. The **spread** of readings will be close together.

I never knew variables could vary so much!

> **Types of variable**

- **Categoric** variables: These have word labels.
  eg. iron wire, copper wire.
- **Ordered** variables: These are categoric variables that we can put into an order. eg. small, medium, large.
- **Discrete** variables: These can only have whole number values.
  eg. number of layers of insulation keeping a beaker warm, 1, 2, 3.
- **Continuous** variables: These can have any numerical value.
  eg. the temperature of water in a beaker, 22.6 °C.

> **Presenting your data in tables**

- **Independent** variable. This is what you change deliberately, step by step.
  It goes in the first column of the table, and on the horizontal axis of a graph.
- **Dependent** variable. This changes as a result.
  It goes in the second column(s) of a table, and on the vertical axis of a graph.
- **Control** variables. These should all be kept constant, so that it is a fair test.

independent variable	dependent variable			
	1st reading	2nd reading	3rd reading	Mean (average)

> **Control variables**

In field studies and tests on living things, it is difficult to control all the variables, so you need to consider control groups and the size of your samples.

▶ Presenting your data on graphs

A graph shows you what the pattern or relationship is between the two variables.

Choose the best type of graph by looking at the **in**dependent variable.
- If it is a continuous variable – use a line-graph.
- If it is a categoric variable – use a bar chart.

▶ Types of line-graph

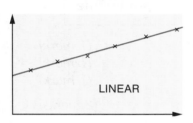

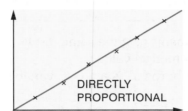

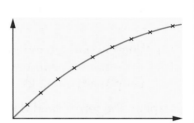

This shows a 'positive linear' relationship. A line sloping down would be 'negative linear'.
The 'line of best fit' gives an average line.
Ignore any **anomalous** *results.*

This graph is a straight line through the origin (0,0).
eg. velocity–time for an object with constant acceleration (Topic 9)
eg. current–voltage for an ohmic conductor (see Topic 14)

eg. velocity–time for a falling object (Topic 10)
eg. current–voltage for a filament lamp (Topic 14)
The graph could curve down, see the half-life graph, Topic 7.

From the pattern of the graph you should be able to draw a conclusion.

▶ Evaluating your investigation

You need to consider the reliability and validity by:
- looking up data from **secondary** sources, eg. on the Internet,
- checking your results by using an alternative method,
- seeing if other people following your method get the same results, ie. are your results reproducible?

▶ Science and society

When making decisions, citizens should look at the evidence, but also ask:
- Is the data **biased**? (eg. from a company with a commercial interest).
- Is political pressure at work?
- Is the scientist experienced, with a good reputation?

New discoveries often raise difficult issues – these can be ethical, social, economic, or environmental issues.

▶ Limitations of Science

There are some questions that Science cannot answer.

Science can answer the question '**How** *can we produce electricity from nuclear fission?*' (see Topic 17), but the question '**Should** *we produce electricity from nuclear fission?*' is for society to decide.

Take care:
- Make sure you are familar with all the **bold** words on these two pages.
- Be clear about the difference between *reliable* and *valid*, and between *accurate* and *precise*.
- When you do your ISAs, make sure that you work carefully and accurately.

There are many more details in **Physics for You**, on pages 6–7 and pages 358–367.

How Science works

Homework Questions

1   Complete the three sentences by choosing the correct word from the box.
    Each word or phrase may be used once or not at all.

biased	categoric	continuous	control	ordered	reproducible

   (a) When two independent experiments give the same results, the data is . . . .   *(1 mark)*
   (b) . . . . variables can have any numerical value.   *(1 mark)*
   (c) A cupboard label, like 'Bunsen burners', is a . . . . variable.   *(1 mark)*

2   Explain the term 'valid data'.   *(2 marks)*

3   Explain why you should always try to repeat a reading if you can.   *(1 mark)*

4   Name two sources of secondary data.   *(2 marks)*

5   State which type of graph would be the best for displaying these sorts of data:
   (a) The temperature of a cup of coffee as time goes on.   *(1 mark)*
   (b) The number of people with blue eyes and the number with brown eyes in
       your class.   *(1 mark)*

6   Emma measures speeds of cars that go past her school. These are her readings:

Car	1	2	3	4	5	6	7	8
Speed of car in m/s	14.0	14.5	13.0	12.5	12.0	15.0	13.0	11.5

   (a) What is the range of speeds in her results?   *(1 mark)*   12
   (b) What is the average speed of the cars?   *(1 mark)*   marks

Examination Questions

1   Amy is measuring the resistance of a LDR. The resistance depends on the amount of light.
    She places a bright lamp 50 cm from the LDR and makes sure that this distance does not
    change.

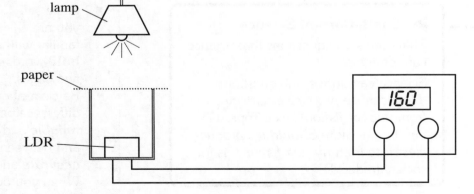

    She notes the resistance and then covers the LDR with a thin sheet of paper. She measures
    the resistance again and then puts another layer of paper over the LDR. She repeats this for
    several more layers of paper.

These are Amy's results:

Number of pieces of paper	0	1	2	3	4	5
Resistance in Ω	100	160	520	410	650	1100

(a) Explain why the distance between the lamp and the LDR is a control variable.

....

(1 mark)

(b) Explain why the number of layers of paper is

    (i)   the independent variable ....

....

    (ii) a discrete variable ....

....

(2 marks)

(c) Plot Amy's results on these axes.

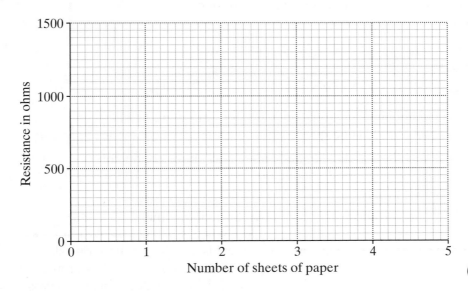

(3 marks)

(d) Amy made a mistake with one reading.
    (i)   Circle the mistaken reading.
    (ii) Draw a line of best fit for the other points.
    (iii) Suggest the correct resistance for the mistaken reading . . . . Ω.   *(3 marks)*

9 marks

2 There is public concern about the level of radioactivity on a beach near a nuclear power station. Jessica and Daniel decide to investigate. Jessica is a scientist. She works for the company that built the power station. Jessica brings precise equipment from her laboratory and takes daily readings for a week. She reports that the level of radioactivity is safe.

Daniel is a journalist, he works for the daily newspaper. He borrows some test equipment, takes one reading and then writes an article headlined 'Seaside Radiation Scare'.

(a) Suggest **two** reasons why Daniel's reading may not be reliable.

....

(b) Suggest **two** reasons why Jessica's report may not be reliable.

....

4 marks

(4 marks)

Answers on page 112

CONDUCTION
CONVECTION
RADIATION

▶ **ThinkAbout:**

1. When a hot object is touching a cold object, energy is transferred from the . . . . object to the . . . . object.
2. Heat can be transferred by conduction, ..., and . . . .

3. Metals are . . . . conductors. Non-metals are usually poor . . . .
4. Air and other gases are . . . . conductors. They are good . . . .
5. Heat can also be called . . . . energy.

▶ Conduction

Conduction is the transfer of energy through a substance without the substance itself moving.

At the hot end the atoms are vibrating with more kinetic energy, and this energy is gradually passed along the bar.

Non-metals, liquids and gases are usually poor conductors. Metals are very good conductors.

Metals are very good conductors because they have a lot of free electrons that can move through the metal.

Heat is transferred more quickly,
* if the conductor is shorter in length,
* if the conductor is bigger in cross-sectional area,
* if the temperature difference is greater.

Ways of reducing the heat loss from a house

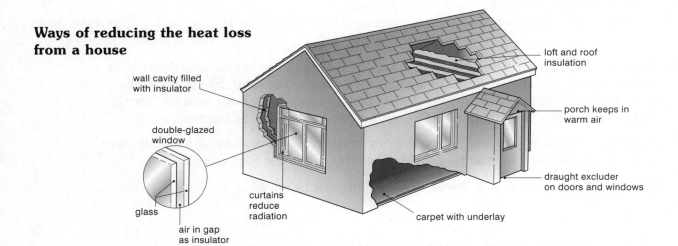

loft and roof insulation

wall cavity filled with insulator

porch keeps in warm air

double-glazed window

draught excluder on doors and windows

glass

curtains reduce radiation

carpet with underlay

air in gap as insulator

Answers:

1. hot, cold   2. convection, radiation   3. good, conductors   4. poor, insulators   5. thermal

► Convection

Liquids and gases can flow, and so they can transfer energy from hot places to colder places.

> The particles in the liquid or gas (fluid) move faster when they are hot. The fluid expands.
>
> The warm regions are then **less dense** than the cold regions. So the warm regions rise, and the colder regions replace the warmer regions.

Warm air is less dense and rises

Cold air is more dense, and falls

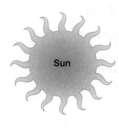
Sun

► Radiation

The hotter an object is, the more energy it radiates, like the Sun.

Hot objects emit mainly **infra-red** radiation.
The energy is transferred by electromagnetic waves (see Topic 6).
Particles of matter are **not** involved.

Emitting

For surfaces at the same temperature, a dark, matt surface **emits more** energy than a light shiny surface.
eg. this is why kettles are shiny, to stay hot.
eg. the warm pipes at the back of a fridge are black, to lose energy.

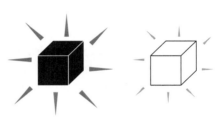

Absorbing

A dark matt surface is also a good **absorber** of radiation energy (because it is a poor reflector).
eg. this is why solar panels are matt black, to absorb as much energy as possible.

A light, shiny surface is a better reflector, so it is a poor absorber.
eg. this is why fire-fighting suits are shiny.

More details in **Physics for You**, pages 40–51, 209, 211, 213.

Take care:

• Don't confuse the words **conduction** and **convection**.

• Remember they both involve particles, but **radiation** does not.

• Don't confuse the words **emission** and **absorption**.

Conduction, Convection, Radiation

Homework Questions

1 Give another name for thermal energy. *(1 mark)*

2 Explain why metals conduct thermal energy well. *(2 marks)*

3 Explain why convection can happen in liquids and gases, but not in solids. *(1 mark)*

4 Polar bears live in very cold conditions.
   Their thick white fur traps air close to their skin.
   (a) Explain how this fur reduces the amount of thermal energy that a polar bear loses.
      (Your answer should mention conduction, convection and radiation.) *(3 marks)*
   (b) Explain why polar bears might overheat if the temperature rises above 20°C. *(1 mark)*

5 Choose a room in your home and write down three ways that heat transfer from
   the room has been reduced so as to keep it warmer in cold weather. *(3 marks)*

6 The water in a kettle is heated using the energy from an electrical element near the bottom.
   (a) Explain how both conduction and convection play a part in transferring
      the energy. *(2 marks)*
   (b) Suggest a reason why kettles are usually coloured white or silver. *(1 mark)*
   (c) Suggest some reasons why the element in an electric kettle is not placed near
      the top. *(2 marks)*

7 Jack wants to improve the insulation in his home by fitting double-glazed windows.
   (a) Explain how double-glazing reduces the heat transferred from a room on a
      cold day. *(1 mark)*
   (b) Suggest some other advantages of double-glazing. *(2 marks)*
   (c) Suggest an experiment that Jack could do to find out whether the amount of
      heat lost from his room really has decreased. *(1 mark)*

20 marks

Examination Question

The drawing shows a baked potato.

(a) The amount of energy radiated by the potato depends on the size and nature of its surface.
    What else affects the amount of energy radiated by the potato?

    ....
    (1 mark)

(b) When potatoes wrapped in aluminium foil are cooked on a barbeque, the foil goes black.
    What effect does this have on the temperature of the potatoes when they are taken off the
    barbeque, compared to that of hot potatoes in clean shiny foil?
    (Give a reason for your answer.)

    Effect: ....

    ....

    Reason: ....

    ....
    (2 marks)

3 marks

Multiple Choice Examination Questions

1 The diagram shows an aluminium heat sink on a microprocessor in a computer. The heat sink stops the microprocessor overheating.

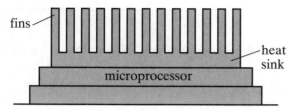

Match words **A**, **B**, **C** and **D** with the spaces **1–4** in the sentences.

A area

B radiation

C conduction

D convection

The heat sink is painted black so that it can emit thermal …**1**… better.

The fins are designed to give the heat sink more surface …**2**…

Air currents rise from the heat sink when energy is transferred by …**3**…

Heat transfer by …**4**… happens easily in a metal like aluminium.

2 Loft insulation in a house is designed to:

A warm the house by increased conduction

B warm the house by increased convection

C reduce energy transfer from the house

D prevent energy transfer into the house

3 Which of these will radiate the most energy?

A a cake in the freezer, at −18°C

B a cake at room temperature, at 18°C

C a cake cooling on a tray, at 80°C

D a cake fresh from the oven, at 180°C

4 Thermal radiation is the transfer of energy by:

A free electrons

B moving air particles

C electromagnetic waves

D sound waves

5 Energy is transferred by conduction when:

A warm air currents rise

B free electrons collide

C waves travel through a vacuum

D pockets of air are trapped

6 Which of these is **not** an effective way to reduce heat loss from a room?

A raising the temperature of the radiators

B fitting double glazed windows

C fitting a thick carpet

D stopping draughts by blocking gaps

7 Which row of the table is correct for different coloured surfaces and thermal radiation?

	best absorber	best emitter
A	matt black	shiny white
B	shiny white	matt black
C	matt black	matt black
D	shiny white	shiny white

8 At 0°C, an iced drink:

A only absorbs thermal radiation

B only emits thermal radiation

C both absorbs and emits thermal radiation

D neither absorbs nor emits thermal radiation

9 Convection cannot happen in solids because:

A solids are good heat insulators

B solids are good heat conductors

C the particles in a solid cannot move

D the particles in a solid cannot flow

10 Which row of the table describes the best duvet to keep you warm in bed?

	type of fibre used	duvet thickness
A	normal	3 cm
B	hollow	5 cm
C	normal	5 cm
D	hollow	3 cm

11 Sam and Megan each buy a cup of coffee. Megan's is in a green china mug, but Sam's is in a blue polystyrene cup and it stays warm longer. This is because:

A different materials transfer heat differently

B polystyrene conducts heat better than china

C convection currents can flow in coffee

D the cups are different colours

Answers on page 112

Energy transfers

> **ThinkAbout:**
>
> 1. Energy is measured in . . . .
> 2. Energy can exist in many different . . . .
>   It can be transferred or transformed from one . . . . to another.
> 3. An electric iron transfers . . . . energy to . . . . energy.
> 4. A match changes . . . . energy to . . . . and . . . . energy.
> 5. A microphone transforms . . . . energy to . . . . energy.
> 6. An electric motor transfers . . . . energy to . . . . energy.

▶ Forms of energy

Energy can exist as heat (thermal energy), sound, light (radiant), electrical, movement (kinetic), nuclear, gravitational potential energy, elastic potential energy, and chemical (food/fuel) energy.

It is measured in joules (J).

In the diagram, gravitational potential energy (PE) is being transferred to kinetic energy (KE):
(To calculate gravitational PE, see Topic 10.)

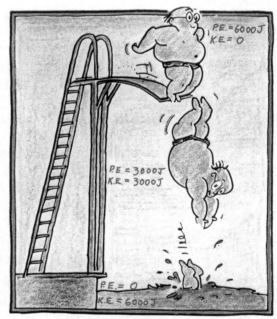

The total energy is constant

▶ Energy Transfer Diagrams

Here is an Energy Transfer Diagram for a torch:

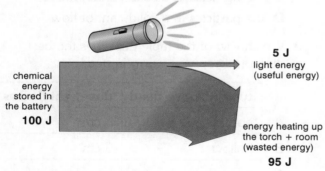

chemical energy stored in the battery
100 J

5 J
light energy (useful energy)

energy heating up the torch + room (wasted energy)
95 J

As you can see, the *total* amount of energy is constant. (100 J = 5 J + 95 J)

Although there is the same amount of energy afterwards, *not all of it is useful*.

Eventually both the 'useful' energy and the 'wasted' energy are transferred to the surroundings, which become warmer.

> **Law 1** (the law of conservation of energy)
> The total amount of energy is constant ('conserved').
> Energy cannot be created or destroyed.

> **Law 2** (the law of spreading of energy)
> In energy transfers, the energy spreads out, to more and more places.
> As it spreads, it becomes less useful to us.

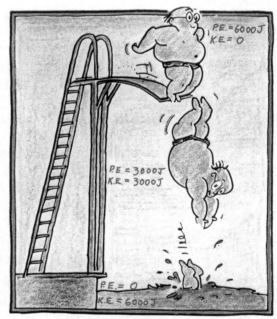

Inside diagram labels: P.E.= 6000 J K.E.= 0 ; P.E.= 3000 J K.E.= 3000 J ; P.E.= 0 K.E.= 6000 J

Answers: 1. joules (J) 2. forms (types), form (type) 3. electrical, heat (thermal) 4. chemical, heat and light 5. sound, electrical 6. electrical, movement (kinetic)

▶ Efficiency

In the torch diagram on the opposite page,
for every 100 joules of energy supplied to the bulb,
only 5 joules are transferred as *useful* light energy.
The rest is wasted.
We say the **efficiency** is $\frac{5}{100}$ or 0.05 or 5%.

The definition of efficiency is:

$$\text{efficiency} = \frac{\text{useful energy transferred (output)}}{\text{total energy supplied (input)}}$$

Example 1

What is the efficiency of this modern
'energy-saver' light bulb?

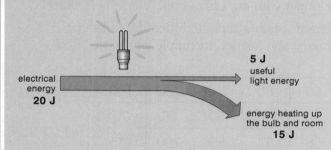

electrical energy
20 J

5 J
useful
light energy

energy heating up
the bulb and room
15 J

$$\text{efficiency} = \frac{\text{useful energy transferred by the bulb}}{\text{total energy supplied to the bulb}}$$

$$= \frac{5}{20}$$

$$= \underline{0.25} \quad \text{or} \quad \underline{25\%}$$

Example 2

A kettle is supplied
with 180 000 joules
of electrical energy,
but 18 000 joules
are lost to the
surroundings.
What is the efficiency of the kettle in heating
the water?

$$\text{useful energy} = 180\ 000\ \text{J} - 18\ 000\ \text{J}$$
$$= 162\ 000\ \text{J}$$

$$\text{efficiency} = \frac{\text{useful energy transferred}}{\text{total energy supplied}}$$

$$= \frac{162\ 000\ \text{J}}{180\ 000\ \text{J}}$$

$$= \underline{0.9} \quad \text{or} \quad \underline{90\%}$$

Example 3 (more difficult)

A solar panel has an efficiency of 15% (= 0.15).
What is its electrical output if the input is 200 W?

In 1 second, the energy supplied is 200 joules.

$$\text{efficiency} = \frac{\text{useful energy transferred}}{\text{total energy supplied}}$$

$$0.15 = \frac{\text{useful energy transferred}}{200\ \text{J}}$$

$$\text{useful energy transferred} = 0.15 \times 200\ \text{J}$$

$$= 30\ \text{J} \quad \text{(in 1 second)}$$

$$\text{so power output} = \underline{30\ \text{W}}$$

Take care:

- There are no units
  for efficiency.
  It is just a number
  (eg. 0.8 or 80%).

- Exam questions may ask you
  to suggest ways of reducing
  wasteful energy transfers.

More details in ***Physics for You***, pages 99–103, 116, 264.

Energy transfers

Homework Questions

1 Name the unit for measuring energy. *(1 mark)*

2 Why is there no unit for efficiency? *(1 mark)*

3 Which form of energy is usually wasted? *(1 mark)*

4 Ngozi listens to music using a wind-up (clockwork) radio.
She winds up a spring which turns a generator as it uncoils.
The generator provides the current for the radio.
Draw a diagram to show all the energy transfers involved.
(Remember that some energy will be wasted during each transfer.) *(5 marks)*

5 A torch is fitted with a LED lamp in place of its normal bulb.
The LED lamp is 12% efficient.
(a) Draw an Energy Transfer Diagram (Sankey Diagram) for the torch. *(3 marks)*
(b) Suggest a reason why the torch battery lasts longer with the LED lamp. *(1 mark)*

6 Sophie tested a pulley system. She attached different weights and lifted them by the same
distance. Each time, she measured how much energy she needed to supply when she lifted
the weight.

Weight lifted (in N)	20	40	60	80	100	120	140
Useful work done (in J)	10	20	30	40	50	60	70
Energy supplied (in J)	25	43	59	73	86	100	115
Efficiency	0.40						0.61

(a) Copy the table and fill in the blank spaces. *(3 marks)*
(b) Name the independent variable and a control variable. *(2 marks)*
(c) Plot a graph of the 'Weight lifted' against the 'Efficiency'. *(4 marks)*
(d) Describe the trend shown in your graph. *(1 mark)*

> *Hint:* Efficiency =
> useful work done ÷
> energy supplied

22
marks

Examination Question

The drawing shows the energy
transferred each second by a
television set.
(a) What form of energy is
    transferred as waste
    energy by the television set?

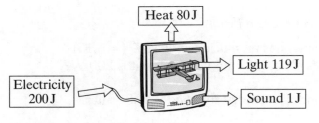

.... *(1 mark)*

(b) What effect will the waste energy have on the air around the television set?

.... *(1 mark)*

(c) Use the following equation to calculate the efficiency of the television set:

efficiency = $\dfrac{\text{useful energy transferred by device}}{\text{total energy supplied to device}}$

....

....

Efficiency = ... **4**

(2 marks) marks

Multiple Choice Examination Questions

1 The diagram shows a digital watch. It is powered by a cell containing silver oxide and zinc.

Match words **A**, **B**, **C** and **D** with the spaces **1–4** in the sentences.

A heat

B electrical

C chemical

D potential

The main energy change in the cell is a transfer of …**1**… energy to …**2**… energy. A small amount of the energy is wasted as …**3**… energy.
Old fashioned watches used the energy stored in a coiled spring, this is called …**4**… energy.

2 Waste energy from a car is sent to the radiator. Eventually, this energy:

A warms the surroundings

B is recycled

C becomes more efficient

D cools the engine

3 Electric motors are never 100% efficient because:

A some energy is always wasted as heat

B electric motors can be very quiet

C some parts of the motor do not move

D there is a force between the magnets

4 When 100 J of gravitational potential energy is transferred it becomes exactly 100 J of other forms of energy. This is because:

A gravitational potential energy depends on height

B gravitational potential energy depends on mass

C energy cannot be wasted

D energy cannot be destroyed

5 The energy transformation (Sankey) diagram is for the engine of a racing motorbike.

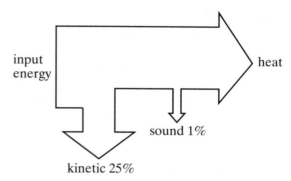

(a) The amount of input energy transferred to heat in the engine is:

A	100%	**B**	74%
C	25%	**D**	1%

(b) The efficiency of the engine is:

A	100%	**B**	74%
C	25%	**D**	1%

6 Which row of the table, A, B, C or D, shows what happens when efficiency increases?

	% useful energy	% wasted energy
A	reduces	increases
B	increases	reduces
C	increases	increases
D	reduces	reduces

7 Calum measures the efficiency of an electric motor when it lifts different weights by the same height. The height is:

A the independent variable

B the dependent variable

C a discrete variable

D a control variable

8 Chloe spends £60 on loft insulation. It saves her £30 each year on heating bills. What is the payback time?

A	6 months	**B**	1 year
C	2 years	**D**	3 years

9 Siân's guitar amplifier can produce up to 120 W of sound. It produces 60 W of heat even when she is not playing. (1 W = 1 J/s)
The efficiency of the amplifier could be:

A	120% at most	**B**	100% at most
C	66% at most	**D**	33% at most

Answers on page 112

Using electricity

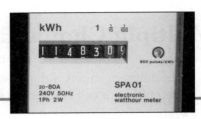

▶ **ThinkAbout:**

1. Movement energy is also called . . . . energy. Heat is also called . . . . energy.
2. A kettle transfers electrical . . . . to . . . . energy.
3. An electric lamp transfers . . . . energy to . . . . and . . . . energy.
4. A loudspeaker transforms . . . . energy to . . . . energy.
5. An electric motor transfers . . . . energy to . . . . energy.
6. A hair-dryer transfers . . . . energy to . . . ., ... and . . . . energy.

▶ **Electrical energy**

Electrical energy is very convenient, and easily transferred to heat, light, sound and kinetic energy in your home.
(For other forms of energy see also Topic 3.)

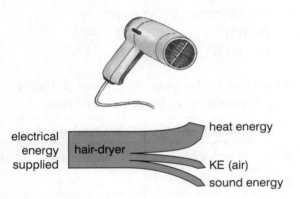

electrical energy supplied → hair-dryer → heat energy, KE (air), sound energy

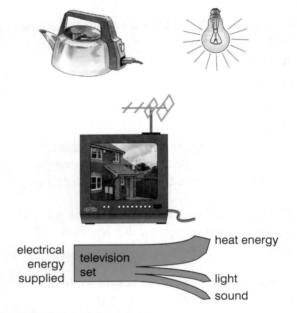

electrical energy supplied → television set → heat energy, light, sound

More examples:

Device:	Electrical energy is transformed to:
Electric fire	Heat, light
Vacuum cleaner motor	Kinetic energy, sound, heat
Loudspeaker in MP3 player	Sound, heat
Electric clock	Kinetic energy, heat
Computer screen	Light, heat

Energy is measured in joules (J).

Power is a measure of how fast the energy is transformed.
The greater the power, the more energy is transformed in a given time.

Power is measured in watts (W) or in kilowatts (kW). 1kW = 1000 watts.

$$\textbf{power} \text{ (in watts, W)} = \frac{\textbf{energy transformed} \text{ (in joules, J)}}{\textbf{time taken} \text{ (in seconds, s)}}$$

See Topic 16 for more details.

▷ Transferring energy

How much electrical energy is transferred by an appliance depends on:

- how much time the appliance is switched on,
- how fast the appliance transfers energy (its *power*).

If the energy is measured in kilowatt-hours (kWh), then the formula is:

> **energy transferred** = **power** × **time**
> (kilowatt-hour, kWh)   (kilowatt, kW)   (hour, h)

The cost of this energy is found by:

> **total cost** = **number of kWh** × **cost per kWh**

Example 1

A 2 kW electric fire is switched on for 5 hours. What is the cost, at 8p per kWh?

energy transferred = power × time
= 2 kW × 5 h
= 10 kWh

cost = number of kWh × cost per kWh
= 10 kWh × 8p per kWh
= 80 pence

Example 2

The number of kWh can be found by reading an electricity meter:

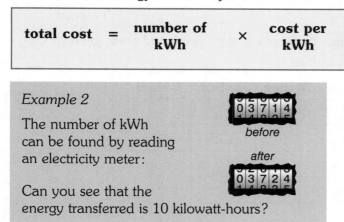

before

after

Can you see that the energy transferred is 10 kilowatt-hours?

▷ The National Grid

Energy is transferred by electricity from a power station to your home along the National Grid.

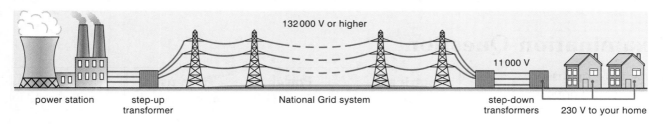

132 000 V or higher

11 000 V

power station   step-up transformer   National Grid system   step-down transformers   230 V to your home

At the power station, a **transformer** is used to step-**up** the voltage (the potential difference).
Increasing the voltage reduces the current.
The smaller current reduces the energy losses in the cables (because there is less heating of the cables).

Near your home, a step-**down** transformer produces a safer voltage (230 V).

For more details see Topic 23.

More details in ***Physics for You***, pages 11, 100, 110, 267, 303.

Take care:

Notice that joules, watts and seconds go together, while kWh, kilowatts and hours go together.

Using electricity

Homework Questions

1   Name the unit for measuring power.   *(1 mark)*

2   Name **two** units for measuring electrical energy.   *(2 marks)*

3   Explain why transformers are used in the National Grid:
    (a) to produce high voltages for transmission,
    (b) to reduce the voltage for use at home.   *(3 marks)*

4   Choose 3 electrical devices that you use in your home, and write down the energy
    transfers that each one is meant to cause when it is working properly.
    (Remember – energy can be wasted.)   *(3 marks)*

5   Tom runs a café and makes lots of toast every day. He needs a new toaster and finds some
    information on the Internet.

Toaster type	2-slice	3-slice	4-slice	6-slice
Power rating in kW	1.2	1.7	2.2	3.0
Slices per hour	65	98	130	195
Energy cost per hour				45 p
Average cost of toasting a slice				0.23 p

Tom's electricity bill shows that 1 kWh costs 15 p.
(a) Copy the table and fill in the blank spaces.   *(6 marks)*
(b) Which toaster uses energy the quickest? Explain why.   *(2 marks)*
(c) Which toaster makes the cheapest toast? Explain why.   *(2 marks)*
(d) Tom chooses the 4-slice toaster. Suggest why he prefers it to a smaller one.   *(1 mark)*
(e) Although the café is very busy, Tom will not need to use the toaster continuously.
    Explain how this might affect the average amount of energy needed to toast a slice.
    (1 mark) $\overline{23}$

6   Most electric trains use a 25 kV power supply. Suggest a reason for this.   *(2 marks)*   marks

Examination Question

In the table opposite,
four electrical appliances
are listed with their power
ratings and the number of
hours they are used
each week.

Electrical appliance	Power ratings (W)	Time used each week (h)	kWh used each week
TV	200	35	
Kettle	2000	2	
Toaster	1000	1	
Cooker	11 500	7	

(a) Complete the table by inserting the number of kWh used by each appliance each week.

(b) Which appliance would cost the least to run per week?

....

(c) The cost of running a toaster is 8 p per week. How much does it cost to run the kettle each
    week? $\overline{6}$

....   *(6 marks)*   marks

Multiple Choice Examination Questions

1 Match words **A**, **B**, **C** and **D** with the spaces **1–4** in the sentences.

   A joule   **B** watt

   C kilowatt   **D** kilowatt hour

Two units for measuring energy are …**1**… and …**2**…

Two units for measuring power are …**3**… and …**4**…

2 Which of these appliances is designed to produce heat?

   A electric drill

   B television

   C microwave oven

   D music player

3 The main purpose of the National Grid is to:

   A connect power stations together

   B connect transformers together

   C supply consumers with electrical energy

   D supply consumers with electricity

4 Which row of the table, **A**, **B**, **C** or **D**, shows the effects of step-up transformers in the National Grid?

	current is	power losses are
A	reduced	increased
B	increased	reduced
C	increased	increased
D	reduced	reduced

5 The diagram shows part of the National Grid.

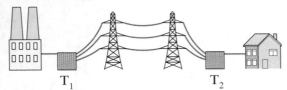

Which row of the table, **A**, **B**, **C** or **D** describes the transformers T_1 and T_2?

	T_1	T_2
A	step-up	step-up
B	step-up	step-down
C	step-down	step-up
D	step-down	step-down

6 Holly noted the total amount of time that she used some electrical appliances during a week.

	appliance	power	time
A	television	100 W	25 hours
B	kettle	3 kW	$\frac{1}{2}$ hour
C	toaster	2 kW	1 hour
D	filament lamp	60 W	30 hours

(a) Which appliance, **A**, **B**, **C** or **D**, used the most energy?

(b) Holly pays 14 p for 1 kWh. How much did it cost her to use the kettle during the week?

   A $\frac{1}{2}$ p   **B** 3 p   **C** 21 p   **D** 42 p

7 Craig compares an electric kettle and a stove by boiling some water using each of them. He notes what happens:

	Kettle	Stove
Amount of water	1.5 litres	1 litre
Time to boil	3 minutes	4 minutes
Power	3 kW	2 kW

(a) Which row of the table, **A**, **B**, **C** or **D**, is a correct conclusion?

	The kettle	The stove
A	uses more energy	boils more quickly
B	uses less energy	boils less quickly
C	uses less energy	boils more quickly
D	uses more energy	boils less quickly

(b) Craig knows that this is not a fair test of the two methods. Which of these is the reason?

   A the times are not the same

   B the power ratings are not the same

   C the amounts of water are not the same

   D Craig has not repeated the experiment

8 The power of a mobile phone charger is 5 W. It takes 5 hours to charge the phone's battery.

The energy transferred is:

   A 0.005 kWh   **B** 0.025 kWh

   C 5 kWh   **D** 25 kWh

Answers on page 113

Generating electricity

▶ **ThinkAbout:**

1. Coal, gas, oil and wood are all . . . .
   They release . . . . when they are burned.
2. Coal, oil and gas are called . . . . fuels.
   Fossil fuels and nuclear fuels are called
   non- . . . . energy resources.

3. Once fosssil fuels are used up, they can
   . . . . be replaced for million years.
4. Wood (biomass) is a . . . . energy resource.
   Other renewable resources are . . . . and
   . . . . and . . . .

▶ **Generating electricity in power stations**

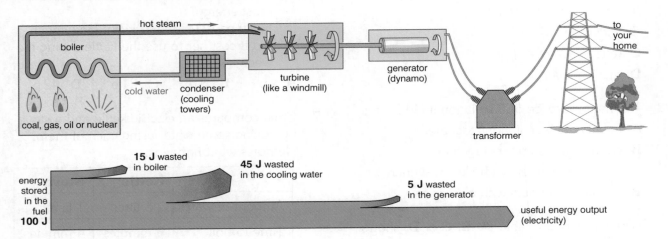

Energy from a fuel is used to heat water.
Fuels include:
- fossil fuels (eg. gas, oil, coal),
- nuclear fuels (eg. uranium, plutonium).
The steam which is produced is used to turn turbines.
The turbines then drive generators, which produce
electricity (see Topic 23).

▶ **Generating electricity from renewable energy resources**

Energy from renewable resources can be used to drive turbines directly, using:
- the wind (eg. a wind generator or a windmill),
- the rise and fall of water due to waves,
- the flow of falling water from a hydroelectric dam, or a tidal barrage.

In some volcanic areas, hot water or steam may rise near to the surface.
The steam can be tapped and used to drive a turbine.
This geothermal energy originally came from the decay of radioactive elements
(eg. uranium) within the Earth.

Electricity can be produced directly from the Sun's radiation, using a solar cell.

Answers:
1. fuels, energy   2. fossil, renewable   3. not   4. renewable, sunlight/wind/waves/falling water/tides

▶ Effect on the environment

Using different energy sources has different effects on the environment.

These effects include:
- possible global warming, due to the greenhouse effect, due to CO_2 emissions,
- acid rain, due to SO_2 emissions,
- radioactive leaks and waste,
- damage to the local ecology.

See the table below.

▶ Availability

Energy sources also differ in when they can become available, to supply a demand for electricity.

Ideally they should have a short start-up time, so that they can respond quickly to a surge in demand.

See the table below.

▶ Comparing power stations

Power station	Disadvantages:	Advantages:
Coal-fired Oil-fired	• emits CO_2, so it increases greenhouse effect • emits SO_2, and so causes acid rain • limited fuel available	• coal will be the last fossil fuel to run out
Gas-fired	• emits CO_2 (but less than coal) • limited fuel available	• quick start-up if there's a sudden demand
Nuclear	• needs disposal of nuclear waste, safely • risk of big accident, like Chernobyl • limited fuel available, slow start-up	• does not produce CO_2 or SO_2, so does not increase greenhouse effect or make acid rain
Wind (turbine)	• needs many large turbines • unsightly, noisy • unreliable, wind does not blow every day	• free energy resource • no air pollution
Hydroelectric (dam)	• impossible in flat or dry regions • floods a large area, affects ecology • expensive to build	• quick to start up if a sudden demand • reliable energy source (in wet regions) • can be used in reverse to store energy • free energy resource • no air pollution
Tidal (barrage)	• needs a place with high tides • affects the ecology of the area • very expensive to build	• reliable (but the tides may not be at the right time for the demand) • free energy resource • no air pollution
Solar cell	• very high cost per Unit of electricity • unreliable (because dependent on weather and daylight)	• good for remote locations (eg. deserts, satellites) or for small amounts of electricity (eg. watches, calculators) • free energy resource • no air pollution

More details in **Physics for You**, pages 14–15 (renewable sources), pages 101, 104 (energy transfers), pages 105–107 (start-up times, costs), page 349 (nuclear power station).

Take care:

To get full marks in exam questions, you may need to refer to more than one advantage / disadvantage.

Generating electricity

Homework Questions

1 Name **three** renewable energy sources. *(3 marks)*

2 Name **three** non-renewable energy sources. *(3 marks)*

3 Draw a diagram to show how the types of energy are transferred
   (a) when a solar cell is working, and
   (b) when a nuclear power station is working. *(4 marks)*

4 Explain how a geothermal power station works. *(4 marks)*

5 State **two** advantages and **two** disadvantages of using nuclear power stations. *(4 marks)*

6 Explain why it is sensible to have
   (a) a reserve of unused power stations, and
   (b) gas-fired power stations as part of this reserve. *(3 marks)*

7 There is a plan to build a tidal power station by damming a large shallow bay near a seaside
   town. Mud flats and a beach, that are normally uncovered twice a day, would be under water
   all the time. There is an alternative plan to build a wind farm along the cliffs very close to
   the town.
   (a) Choose either of the schemes and state **two** environmental reasons in favour of
       choosing it. *(2 marks)*
   (b) State **two** environmental reasons for rejecting the scheme you did not choose. *(2 marks)*
   (c) Describe another way to generate electricity that uses energy from the sea. *(1 mark)*

8 Fifty years ago, most of the power stations in the United Kingdom used coal.
   Nowadays, only about a third of our electricity comes from coal-fired power stations.
   Suggest why this change has happened by giving
   (a) some technical developments that have made it possible, and
   (b) some environmental considerations that are seen as more important nowadays. *(4 marks)*

30
marks

Examination Question

(a) The bar chart shows the start-up times
   for different types of fuel-burning
   power stations.

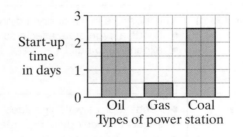

   Which type of power station would be
   the quickest to start producing electricity?

   .... *(1 mark)*

(b) A fuel-burning power station is more reliable than a wind generator at producing
   electricity. Explain why.

   ....

   ....

   .... *(2 marks)*

(c) Fuel-burning power stations may produce air pollution. Why does a wind generator
   not produce any air pollution?

   ....

   .... *(1 mark)*

4
marks

Multiple Choice Examination Questions

1 The diagram shows a device that uses energy from the wind to produce electricity.

Match words **A**, **B**, **C** and **D** with the spaces **1–4** in the sentences.

A generator   **B** renewable
C turbine   **D** variable

The wind turns the ...**1**... and then the ...**2**... transfers the energy to electricity.
An advantage of using the wind is that it is a ...**3**... energy source.
A disadvantage of using the wind is that it supplies a ...**4**... amount of energy.

2 The energy transfer in a solar cell is:
A from thermal energy to electrical energy
B from light energy to electrical energy
C from electrical energy to light energy
D from electrical energy to thermal energy

3 An advantage of a nuclear power station is:
A it produces radioactive waste
B it is expensive to decommission
C it produces no greenhouse gases
D it contains hazardous material

4 Which of these power stations does not need a steam turbine?
A nuclear power station
B gas-fired power station
C geothermal power station
D tidal power station

5 Which row of the table, **A**, **B**, **C** or **D**, correctly shows the energy sources for coal-fired and hydroelectric power stations?

	coal-fired	hydroelectric
A	fossil fuel	fossil fuel
B	renewable energy	fossil fuel
C	renewable energy	renewable energy
D	fossil fuel	renewable energy

6 In a hydroelectric power station:
A moving water turns a turbine
B water is heated to turn a turbine
C a large amount of cooling water is needed
D decommissioning costs are a concern

7 Which of these is a true statement about hydroelectricity?
A it provides free electricity
B it does not work at night
C it causes environmental damage
D it produces polluting gas when it is working

8 Karen would like to use solar cells, instead of a mains charger, for her batteries. Which row of the table, **A**, **B**, **C** or **D**, compares the costs correctly?

	Initial cost higher	Running cost lower
A	for solar cells	for mains charger
B	for mains charger	for mains charger
C	for mains charger	for solar cells
D	for solar cells	for solar cells

9 An advantage of a gas-fired power station is:
A it produces carbon dioxide (a greenhouse gas)
B it can be started up quickly
C it uses renewable energy
D it releases heat into the atmosphere

10 Jim spends £400 a year on electricity. A small wind turbine would cost him £1000, but could supply half his electricity needs for no further cost.
(a) What is the payback time for the wind turbine?

A 1 year   **B** $2\frac{1}{2}$ years
C 5 years   **D** 10 years

(b) If the cost of electricity rises, Jim would find:
A he would need to buy a faster turbine
B he would have to use the turbine less
C the payback time would become longer
D the payback time would become shorter

Answers on page 113

Getting the Grades – Energy

Try this question, then compare your answer with the two examples opposite ▶

The graph shows the expected change in the world demand for energy.
It also shows how the supplies of various energy resources are expected to change.

Energy

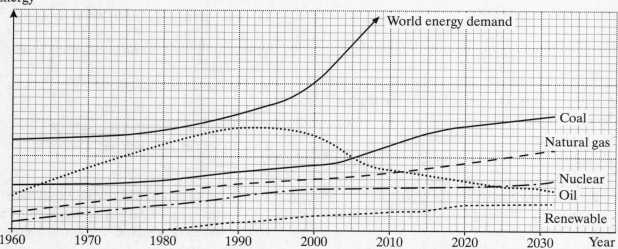

(a) The supply of energy from oil is decreasing. The supply from coal is increasing.

   (i) Why is this a problem for the environment?

   .... *(1 mark)*

   (ii) Use the graph to estimate when supplies from oil and coal are equal. .... *(1 mark)*

(b) We have relied on fossil fuels to supply most of our energy needs.
   Use the graph to explain why:

   (i) there could be a supply problem in the future:

   .... *(1 mark)*

   (ii) we must find alternative energy resources.

   .... *(1 mark)*

(c) On average, the energy use of each family in the UK releases over 25 tonnes of
carbon dioxide and 4 kilograms of sulfur dioxide into the air *every year*.

   (i) State one environmental effect which is increased by releasing carbon dioxide into the
atmosphere.

   .... *(1 mark)*

   (ii) State a different environmental effect caused by releasing sulfur dioxide into the atmosphere.

   .... *(1 mark)*

(d) Electricity can be generated using nuclear fuels. Apart from the cost of electricity, what are
the advantages and disadvantages of doing this?

....

.... *(5 marks)*

11

marks

GRADE 'A' ANSWER

Jessica has scored both marks. She gives a complete answer to the first part and correctly reads the graph for the second part.

Jessica correctly answers both parts of the question.

Jessica

(a) (i) coal produces more CO_2 than oil ✓
    (ii) 2005 ✓
(b) (i) The World demand for energy is rising rapidly. ✓
    (ii) Fossil fuels will run out over the next two hundred years, so there will not be enough resources to meet the future demand. ✓
(c) (i) Greenhouse effect causing the earth to get warmer. ✓
    (ii) acid rain ✓
(d) There are plenty of nuclear fuel in the world. ✓ Nuclear power stations do not burn fuels so no waste gases are produced. ✓ Nuclear fuels are radioactive and need to be handled very carefully. ✓ Waste nuclear fuel remains very reactive for a long time and has to be stored away from people. ✓ Nuclear fuels won't run out for a long time. Nuclear fuel can be very unsafe.

Jessica has understood the relationship between energy demand and energy supply and has mentioned both of these in her answer.

Jessica has made four valid points but her last points are really saying the same thing as her previous points so she does not get any extra credit for them.
She could have gained more marks by saying that very little radiation escapes when a nuclear power station is running normally, or that a nuclear power station takes a long time to start up.

10 marks = Grade A answer

▶ Improve your Grades   A up to A*

To get an A* you must be able to argue a clear case without repeating yourself. If there are 5 marks available you must make 5 clear points. You must remember to include both advantages and disadvantages to gain all the marks.

GRADE 'C' ANSWER

Michael does not get any marks because he has not answered the question. Burning oil and coal both cause atmospheric pollution. Michael needs to say that coal produces more CO_2 than oil for the same energy.

Michael scores the first mark, but his answer to the second part is incomplete. He should say that there will not be anough fossil fuels to meet the demand in the future.

Michael

(a) (i) Burning coal causes pollution ✗
    (ii) 2005 ✓

(b) (i) The demand for energy is increasing. ✓
    (ii) Soon there will not be enough. ✗

(c) (i) Damages the ozone layer. ✗
    (ii) Acid rain ✓

(d) Nuclear radiation is dangerous if radioactive substances excape into the environment they will kill things. ✓ The waste is radioactive. ✓ Radioactive waste has to be stored underground. ✓ It takes a long time to start it up.

Michael has read correctly from the graph and scores the mark.

Michael is confused between different problems caused by atmospheric pollution and the first answer is incorrect.

Michael has seen the word 'disadvantages' and has answered accordingly. However, he has forgotten to give any advantages so he cannot gain more than 3 marks. Michael scores 3 of the 5 marks.

6 marks = Grade C answer

▶ Improve your Grades   C up to B

Grade C candidates often fail to get marks because they do not read the questions carefully enough. Make sure that you give a complete answer to each part of the question.

The electromagnetic spectrum

▷ **ThinkAbout:**

1. White light through a prism gives a . . . .
2. The colours of the spectrum are . . . .
3. The frequency of a wave is the number of complete vibrations in one . . . .
4. The wavelength of a wave is the . . . . from one peak (or trough) to the next.

Waves transfer energy from one place to another. For any wave:

> **wave speed = frequency × wavelength**
> (m/s) (hertz, Hz) (metre, m)

Example

Some radio waves with a frequency of 300 000 Hz have a wavelength of 1000 m. What is their speed?

wave speed = frequency × wavelength
= 300 000 Hz × 1000 m
= 300 000 000 m/s

▷ **The full electromagnetic spectrum**

Visible light is just part of the full electromagnetic spectrum:

All these types of electromagnetic wave travel at the same speed through space (a vacuum).

Different wavelengths are reflected, absorbed or transmitted differently by different substances.

When the radiation is absorbed, the energy it carries:
- makes the substance hotter (eg. when you sunbathe),
- may create an alternating current of the same frequency as the radiation (eg. in a radio aerial),
- may cause damage to living cells.

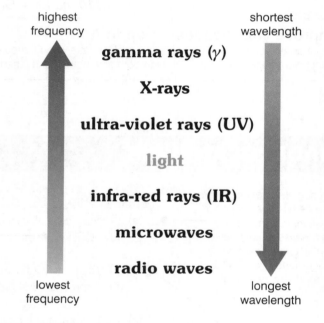

highest frequency — shortest wavelength

gamma rays (γ)

X-rays

ultra-violet rays (UV)

light

infra-red rays (IR)

microwaves

radio waves

lowest frequency — longest wavelength

▷ **The effects of radiation on living cells**

- **Microwaves** are absorbed by the water in cells in your body. The cells may be killed or damaged by the heat released.
- **Infra-red radiation** (IR) is absorbed by the skin and is felt as heat.
- **Ultra-violet radiation** (UV) can pass through the skin to deeper tissues. The darker the skin, the more it absorbs, and less reaches deeper tissues.
- **X-rays** and **gamma rays** (γ) mostly pass through soft tissues, but some is absorbed by the cells, which they may damage (see Topic 7).

High doses of UV, X-rays and γ-radiation can kill normal cells.
Lower doses of these radiations can cause normal cells to become cancerous.

Take care:

Be clear that the shorter the wavelength, the higher the frequency (and usually more dangerous).

Answers: 1. spectrum 2. red, orange, yellow, green, blue, indigo, violet (ROY G BIV) 3. second 4. distance

▷ Uses of electromagnetic waves

Type of radiation	Uses:	More details in *Physics for You*
Gamma rays (γ)	• to kill harmful bacteria in food • to sterilise surgical instruments • to kill cancer cells	• page 347 • page 210
X-rays	• to produce shadow pictures of materials that X-rays do not easily pass through, including bones and metals	• pages 212, 210, 312
Ultra-violet (UV)	• in sun-beds • in fluorescent tube lamps, and security coding. (Special coatings absorb the UV and emit the energy as light.)	• pages 212, 210 • page 212
Visible light	• to see this page; for plants to grow, etc. • in optical fibre communications	• page 192
Infra-red (IR)	• in grills, toasters and radiant heaters • in optical fibre communications • for the remote control of TV sets, etc.	• page 211 • page 192
Microwaves	• to send signals to and from satellites and within mobile phone networks (they pass through the atmosphere) • for cooking, because these wavelengths are strongly absorbed by water molecules in the food	• pages 314, 155 • page 211
Radio waves	• to transmit radio and TV programmes between places on the Earth's surface. (Longer waves can be reflected from the ionosphere, to go round the bend of the Earth.)	• page 221

▷ Communications

Information signals can be sent over long distances via radio waves, cables, or optical fibres.
The signals can be sent as **analogue** signals or as **digital** signals (see the left-hand diagrams below).
Digital signals are used in optical fibres, and can be processed by computers.

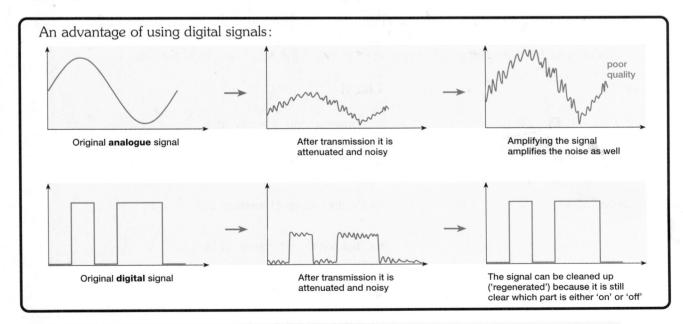

An advantage of using digital signals:

Original **analogue** signal — After transmission it is attenuated and noisy — Amplifying the signal amplifies the noise as well (poor quality)

Original **digital** signal — After transmission it is attenuated and noisy — The signal can be cleaned up ('regenerated') because it is still clear which part is either 'on' or 'off'

More details in *Physics for You*, pages 208–219, 347.

The electromagnetic spectrum

Homework Questions

1 Name the unit for measuring frequency. *(1 mark)*

2. Explain why it is a good idea to use skin cream that absorbs ultra-violet waves when you are outside on a very sunny day. *(2 marks)*

3 Three types of wave, gamma rays, light waves, and infra-red waves all hit the surface of the water in a pond.
(a) Which type of wave has the highest frequency? *(1 mark)*
(b) Which type of wave has the longest wavelength? *(1 mark)*
(c) Explain what happens to each type of wave after it hits the water. *(3 marks)*

4 Microwave ovens are used for cooking food. Explain why:
(a) the food in a microwave oven gets very hot,
(b) a microwave oven can cook food much more quickly than an ordinary oven, and
(c) the glass panel in the door of a microwave oven always contains a metal mesh. *(3 marks)*

5 Explain why microwaves are used instead of radio waves for communicating with a satellite. *(2 marks)*

6 Radio waves travel about a million times faster than sound waves. If a radio wave and a sound wave happen to have the same wavelength, then their frequencies must be different. Explain how and why the two frequencies are different. *(2 marks)*

7 The radio wave for a DAB (Digital Audio Broadcast) transmission has a frequency of 226 million hertz (226 000 000 Hz). The radio wave travels at 300 million m/s (300 000 000 m/s).
(a) Calculate the wavelength of the radio wave. *(3 marks)*
(b) Explain the difference between a digital and an analogue signal. *(2 marks)*
(c) Explain why it is easier to remove noise from digital signals. *(1 mark)*

21 marks

Examination Question

List **A** gives six types of electromagnetic radiation.
List **B** gives some of the uses of electromagnetic radiation.
Draw a straight line from each type of radiation to its use. One has been done for you.

List A	List B
radio waves	to communicate via satellites
microwaves	to communicate with a ship at sea
infra-red rays	to sterilise surgical instruments
ultra-violet rays	to take shadow pictures of bones
X-rays	to see security markings
gamma rays	to change TV channels

(5 marks) 5 marks

Multiple Choice Examination Questions

1   The diagram shows part of the electromagnetic spectrum:

gamma rays	X-rays	ultra-violet rays	visible light	radio waves

Match words **A**, **B**, **C** and **D** with the spaces **1–4** in the sentences.

A gamma ray

B radio wave

C speed

D energy

In space, all electromagnetic waves have the same …**1**…
A …**2**… has the shortest wavelength and a …**3**… has the lowest frequency.
X-rays can be dangerous because people may be harmed by their …**4**…

2   Which row of the table, **A**, **B**, **C** or **D**, describes all types of electromagnetic radiation?

	Move as waves?	Carry energy?
A	yes	yes
B	no	no
C	yes	no
D	no	yes

3   When the energy from radio waves is absorbed by an aerial:

A the whole aerial vibrates

B gamma rays are produced

C a direct current is produced

D an alternating current is produced

4   Which of these is **not** used for communication?

A radio waves   **B** visible light

C infra-red waves   **D** X-rays

5   Which row of the table, **A**, **B**, **C** or **D**, is correct for digital and analogue signals?

	analogue signals	digital signals
A	are only on or off	vary continuously
B	vary continuously	are only on or off
C	are only on or off	are only on or off
D	vary continuously	vary continuously

6   Which of these electromagnetic radiations will travel along an optical fibre?

A radio waves

B infra-red rays

C microwaves

D gamma rays

7   Liam is sunbathing. His skin is absorbing safe amounts of infra-red and ultra-violet rays.
(a) Which row of the table, **A**, **B**, **C** or **D**, shows their effects on his skin?

	infra-red rays	ultra-violet rays
A	cause heating	cause tanning
B	cause tanning	cause tanning
C	cause heating	cause heating
D	cause tanning	cause heating

(b) If Liam forgot to use sunblock cream, then the ultra-violet rays might:

A cause cell mutations leading to bone cancer

B cause cell mutations leading to skin cancer

C heat his brain and cause a tumour

D reflect from his skin and prevent him tanning

8   Visible light waves travel in straight lines, but they will pass along a bent optical fibre because:

A they are reflected inside the fibre

B they are refracted inside the fibre

C they slow down enough to change direction

D they are absorbed by the fibre

9   Microwaves are used for communicating with a satellite over the ocean because they can:

A travel at the same speed as light

B cause heating in materials like water

C pass through the Earth's atmosphere

D also be used in mobile phone networks

10 Microwave transmissions from satellites tend to use digital signals rather than analogue signals. This is because analogue signals:

A are more prone to interference

B are only on or off

C cannot pass through the Earth's atmosphere

D travel more slowly

RADIOACTIVITY

▶ ThinkAbout:

1. Some substances, like uranium, give out
. . . . all the time.
They are said to be . . . .

2. They give out 3 kinds of radiation, called
. . . . and . . . . and . . . .
The most penetrating of these is . . . .

▶ Alpha, beta and gamma rays

There are 3 types of radiation given out
(randomly) by radioactive sources:

- **alpha (α) radiation.** Easily absorbed,
by paper or a few centimetres of air.
An α-particle is a helium nucleus.

- **beta radiation (β)**
Passes through air or paper, but is mostly
absorbed by a few millimetres of metal.
A β-particle is an electron that is emitted
by the nucleus.

- **gamma (γ) radiation**
Very penetrating, needs centimetres of lead
or metres of concrete to absorb most of it.
γ-rays are electromagnetic waves (see Topic 6).

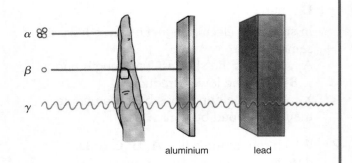

aluminium   lead

Alpha and beta particles are deflected
by both electric and magnetic fields,
but gamma waves are not.

▶ Atomic structure

An atom has a nucleus (which is made
of protons and neutrons).
It is surrounded by electrons.
α, β and γ rays come from the nucleus.

All atoms of an element have the **same**
number of protons. All atoms of
Helium have 2 protons as shown:

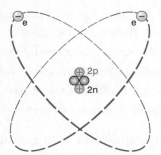

Atoms of the same element can have
different numbers of neutrons. These
are **isotopes**. See Topic 17 (page 78).

▶ Effects of radiation on living tissue

When α, β or γ rays collide with neutral atoms,
these may become *ionised* (charged). In living cells
this ionisation can cause damage, including cancer.
The larger the dose of radiation, the greater the risk.

When the source of radiation is *outside* the body,
- beta and gamma rays are the most dangerous
because they can reach cells, to damage them,
- alpha rays are likely to be stopped by the air or
your outer skin or clothing.

When the source of radiation is *inside* the body,
- alpha radiation is the most dangerous, because
it is strongly absorbed, and strongly ionises,
- beta and gamma rays are less dangerous, as
they are absorbed less and are less ionising.

Very high doses of radiation can be used to kill
cancer cells and harmful microorganisms.

Answers: 1. radiation, radioactive   2. alpha (α), beta (β), gamma (γ); gamma

▶ Half-life

As time goes by, the activity of a radioactive substance decreases.

The half-life:
- is the time taken for the number of parent atoms in a sample to halve,
- is also the time it takes for the count rate to fall to half of its initial level.

You can find the half-life from a graph, by seeing how long it takes for the activity to fall to half.

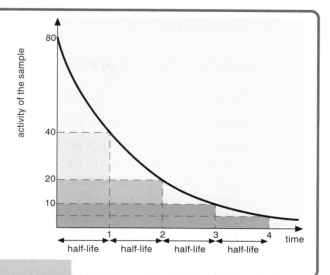

Example

The activity of some iodine-131 is 80 counts/minute. The half-life is 8 days. What is the activity after 24 days?

After 8 days (1 half-life), the activity is 40 counts/min.
After 16 days (2 half-lives), the activity is 20 counts/min.
After 24 days (3 half-lives), the activity is 10 counts/min.

▶ Some uses of radiation

- **Thickness control**
  The thicker the material, the more the radiation is absorbed.
  This can be used to control the rollers to give the correct thickness:

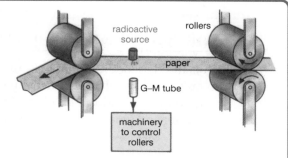

- **Tracers**
  Tracers can be used to track leaks in a pipeline:

  They can also be used as medical tracers in hospitals.

▶ Using the correct radioactive source

In the pipeline shown above, it is important to use the correct radioactive isotope, so that:
- It has a half-life of only a few hours or days. This is so that it remains long enough to be detected, but not so long that it remains a safety problem.
- It is a beta-emitter. Alpha particles would be absorbed by the soil, whereas gamma-rays would pass through the metal pipe anyway.

Take care:

- Be clear about the 3 types of radiation, and their effect on the body.

- You need to be able to evaluate both the *uses* and the *dangers* of radioactivity.

More details in **Physics for You**, pages 340–344, 346–347, 350.

Radioactivity

Homework Questions

1 What is the unit for measuring the activity of a radioactive sample? *(1 mark)*

2 Name **three** types of radiation emitted by radioactive materials. *(3 marks)*

3 Ryan is designing a suit to protect workers at a nuclear plant.
He thinks that he has found some cloth that will absorb gamma rays.
(a) Explain how he could test the cloth to see if he is right. *(3 marks)*
(b) Give a reason why Ryan is probably wrong about the cloth. *(1 mark)*

4 Ellen's house is in a place where there is natural radioactivity in the ground. A radioactive gas seeps from the ground into the house. The gas has a half-life of 3.8 days and it emits alpha particles. Ellen's smoke alarm also emits alpha particles. She is very concerned about the possible dangers.
(a) Describe an alpha particle. *(2 marks)*
(b) Explain why the alpha particles from the smoke alarm are unlikely to cause Ellen harm. *(2 marks)*
(c) The alpha particles from the gas are more likely to be a danger to her, explain why. *(2 marks)*
(d) Explain what is meant by a half-life of 3.8 days. *(2 marks)*

5 A teacher measures the activity of a sample of radon. These are the results:

Time in seconds	0	30	60	90	120	150	180	210	240
Count rate (per second)	206	143	99	69	48	33	23	16	12

(a) Which is the dependent variable in this investigation? *(1 mark)*
(b) Plot a graph to show how the activity of the sample decayed. *(3 marks)*
(c) Use your graph to find the half-life of the sample. *(2 marks)*
(d) Suggest a reason why the activity did not fall to zero. *(2 marks)*

24 marks

Examination Question

A detector and counter are used in an experiment to show that a radioactive source gives out alpha and beta radiation only.
Two different types of absorber are placed one at a time between the detector and the source.
For each absorber, a count is taken over 10 minutes and the average number of counts per second worked out.
The results are shown in the table.

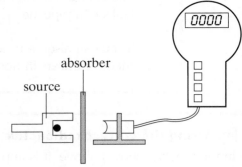

source   absorber

Absorber used	Average counts per second
no absorber	33
card 1 mm thick	20
metal 3 mm thick	2

Explain how these results show that alpha and beta radiation are being given out, but gamma radiation is not being given out.

....

....

....
(3 marks)

3 marks

Multiple Choice Examination Questions

1 The diagram shows the basic structure of the atom.

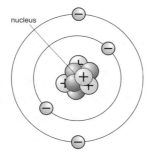

Match words **A**, **B**, **C** and **D** with the spaces **1–4** in the sentences.

A isotopes   **B** neutrons

C protons   **D** electrons

…**1**… are the particles that surround the nucleus of the atom.
The nucleus contains both …**2**… and …**3**…
Atoms of the same element that have different numbers of neutrons are called …**4**…

2 A radioactive substance emits radiation:

A from its nuclei

B half of the time

C until its half-life is over

D for the first half of its life

3 An alpha particle is the same as

A an electron   **B** a gamma ray

C a hydrogen nucleus   **D** a helium nucleus

4 Which row of the table, **A**, **B**, **C** or **D**, is correct for radiation moving in a magnetic field?

	alpha particles are	beta particles are
A	deflected	not deflected
B	not deflected	deflected
C	deflected	deflected
D	not deflected	not deflected

5 Which row of the table, **A**, **B**, **C** or **D**, is correct for radiation moving in an electric field?

	alpha particles are	gamma rays are
A	deflected	not deflected
B	not deflected	deflected
C	deflected	deflected
D	not deflected	not deflected

6 The diagram shows four different radioactive sources, **A**, **B**, **C** and **D**, and how the radiation is affected by some materials of different thickness.

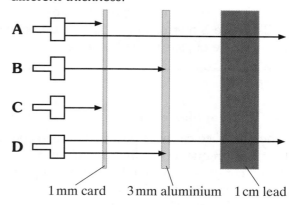

(a) Which source, **A**, **B**, **C** or **D**, is emitting beta particles and gamma rays?

(b) Which source, **A**, **B**, **C** or **D**, would be the safest to use in a smoke alarm at home?

7 The activity of a radioactive source is 32 counts per second. After three half-lives the activity will be:

A 96 counts per second

B 16 counts per second

C 8 counts per second

D 4 counts per second

8 Gamma rays become less dangerous as you move further from the source. This is because the gamma rays:

A are absorbed by a few metres of air

B slow down as they move away from the source

C move apart as they move away from the source

D have a very short half-life

9 Gamma rays are used for:

A treating cancer patients

B monitoring the thickness of sheet metal

C producing energy in nuclear power stations

D cooking food

10 Which of these causes the most ionisation?

A an alpha particle

B a beta particle

C a gamma ray

D an electron

Answers on page 114

The origins of the Universe

▶ **ThinkAbout:**

1. The colours of the spectrum are . . . .
2. There is a force of . . . . attraction between all the objects in the Universe.
3. The Universe is thought to have started in the Big . . . .   The Universe is still . . . .
4. To observe distant stars we use a . . . .

▶ The Doppler effect

When a police car goes past you at high speed, the pitch (frequency) of the siren changes.
As the car goes away, the frequency is lower and the wavelength is longer:
This is called the Doppler effect.

The same effect occurs with light waves.
If an object (eg. a star) goes away from us at high speed, the light is slightly redder.
This is called the **Red-Shift**.

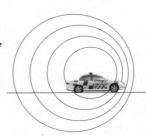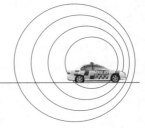

As the car approaches, the wavelength is shorter, and the frequency higher. This means:
- *a higher pitch of sound*
- *a bluer colour of light*

As the car goes away, the wavelength is longer, and the frequency lower. This means:
- *a lower pitch of sound*
- *a redder colour of light*

▶ Observing galaxies

Edwin Hubble used a telescope to observe distant galaxies.
He found that the light from them has a red-shift (a longer wavelength).
So the galaxies are moving away from us, at high speed.

He found that:
- the further away the galaxies are, the bigger the red-shift,
- so the farther galaxies are moving away from us faster than nearer galaxies,
- and it is the same in all directions.

Spectrum of light from our Sun.

Light from a distant galaxy is red-shifted:

red-shift

The dark lines in the spectrum have all shifted towards the red end

This means that the whole Universe is expanding, just like the dots on a balloon move farther apart as the balloon expands:
(The farther apart two dots are, the faster they move apart.)

▶ The Big Bang theory

The expanding Universe means that in the past the Universe started from a single point, which burst apart, producing all matter, energy, space and time.

The Universe has been expanding ever since, against the pull of gravity between the galaxies.

The age of the Universe can be estimated from the current rate of expansion. It is almost 14 billion years old.

An artist's impression of the Big Bang, when our Universe was formed

▶ Observing the Universe

To observe the Universe we use telescopes. The most common ones are:
- Optical telescopes, using visible light. Large mirrors collect the faint light from distant galaxies.
- Radio telescopes, using radio waves:

Because the Earth's atmosphere is dirty, we get better results if these telescopes are launched into space.

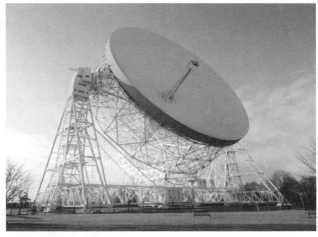

Jodrell Bank radio telescope
The large dish collects radio waves emitted by distant stars

Stars, galaxies and black holes emit electromagnetic waves across the full spectrum (see Topic 6). Each wavelength gives us different information about the Universe.
However, most wavelengths are absorbed by the Earth's atmosphere. So telescopes for
– gamma-rays,
– X-rays,
– ultra-violet (UV)
– infra-red (IR)
have to be launched into space, so they are above the atmosphere.

More details in **Physics for You**, pages 158, 215.

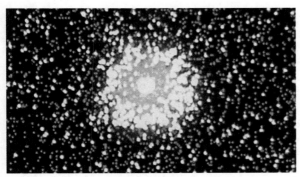

An X-ray photo of Quasar 3C 273.
It is moving away from us at a sixth of the speed of light.

Take care:
- Be clear about the evidence for the expanding Universe, and how this suggests the Big Bang theory.
- Make sure you know about the electromagnetic spectrum (see Topic 6).

The origin of the Universe

Homework Questions

1 Name the theory that suggests that the Universe is expanding. *(1 mark)*

2 Which observation supports this theory? *(1 mark)*

3 How does the wavelength of the light coming from a galaxy relate to the distance between the galaxy and the Earth? *(2 marks)*

4 Explain the advantages and disadvantages of using a space telescope for astronomy, instead of using a telescope on the Earth. *(4 marks)*

5 Light from distant galaxies is observed to have a red-shift.
Explain how the red-shift affects
(a) the wavelength of the light waves, and
(b) the frequency of the light waves. *(2 marks)*

6 A galaxy emits red-shifted light. It also emits radio waves and X-rays.
(a) What information can be deduced about the movement of the galaxy? *(1 mark)*
(b) How will this movement affect the radio waves and the X-rays? *(1 mark)*

7 In a collapsing Universe (one where the galaxies are getting closer together), the wavelength of light from distant objects might be changed.
Explain what would happen to the wavelength of the light and suggest a name for this effect. *(2 marks)*

8 Vesto Slipher measured the red-shift in the light from several galaxies. Edwin Hubble measured the distances between those galaxies and the Earth. These results showed a trend that was the basis for a theory. The theory has since become accepted, despite a lot of inaccuracy in their measurements.
(a) Why has the theory become accepted? *(2 marks)*
(b) How can scientists improve the accuracy of their measurements? *(2 marks)*

18 marks

Examination Question

The 'big bang' theory is one theory of the origin of the Universe.
(a) Explain what is meant by the 'big bang' theory.

....

....

....
(2 marks)

(b) One piece of evidence for the 'big bang' theory is 'red-shift'.
(i) What is 'red-shift'?

....

....
(1 mark)

(ii) Explain how 'red-shift' leads to the 'big bang' theory.

....

....
(4 marks)

7 marks

Multiple Choice Examination Questions

1 Match words **A**, **B**, **C** and **D** with the spaces **1–4** in the sentences.

   A big bang

   B red-shift

   C galaxy

   D X-ray

Some telescopes are designed to detect an invisible type of wave called ...**1**...
A ...**2**... is a cluster of billions of stars. Astronomers have discovered a ...**3**... in the light from distant stars; this supports the ...**4**... theory.

2 Which of these is not emitted by stars and detected with a telescope?

   A X-rays

   B light rays

   C radio waves

   D sound waves

3 Which of these explains why astronomers may prefer to use a space telescope?

   A it produces clear images

   B it is constantly moving

   C it is nearer to the stars

   D it does not work at night

4 Light from the most distant galaxies has:

   A a small red-shift

   B a large red-shift

   C a small blue-shift

   D a large blue-shift

5 Which row of the table, **A**, **B**, **C** or **D**, is correct for light waves from a distant galaxy that is moving away, compared to light from a source on Earth?

	wavelength	frequency
A	seems bigger	seems bigger
B	seems smaller	seems smaller
C	seems bigger	seems smaller
D	seems smaller	seems bigger

6 Which of these is evidence that the Universe is expanding?

   A Most galaxies are moving away from the Earth.

   B Some galaxies are moving towards the Earth.

   C Our Solar System is a tiny part of a galaxy.

   D Many people accept the 'Big Bang' theory.

7 Most astronomers accept that the 'Big Bang' theory is correct because:

   A Edwin Hubble explained his ideas very clearly

   B it fits very well with the evidence we have

   C every galaxy has the same red-shift

   D there are no other theories about the Universe

8 Earth-based telescopes produce slightly fuzzy images because:

   A the Earth spins round once a day

   B there are always slight tremors in the ground

   C the light is affected by the atmosphere

   D the light is affected by radiation from rocks

9 As a galaxy moves away from us, the light waves from it are

   A stretched apart

   B squashed together

   C slowed down

   D speeded up

10 The 'big bang' theory states that the Universe began as:

   A a cluster of galaxies

   B a single galaxy

   C a giant star

   D a single point

11 A noisy racing car moves quickly away from the spectators. They hear the exhaust note. Compared to the sound that the driver hears, the sound that the spectators hear will be:

   A higher pitched

   B lower pitched

   C travelling more quickly

   D travelling more slowly

Answers on page 114

Getting the Grades – Waves and Radiation

Try this question, then compare your answer with the two examples opposite ▶

(a) The diagram shows, in a simplified form, how a telephone call can be transmitted from Britain to the USA.

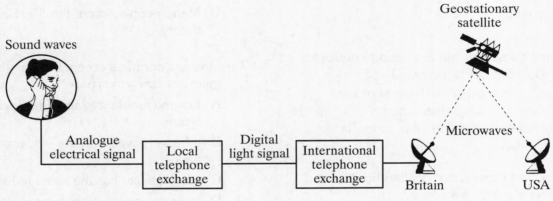

(i) What is the difference between an analogue and a digital signal?

....

.... *(2 marks)*

(ii) Explain why the quality of an analogue signal transmitted over a long distance decreases, but the quality of a digital signal transmitted over the same distance does not change.

....

....

.... *(3 marks)*

(iii) Explain why microwaves are used instead of radio waves to communicate between the satellite and the ground.

....

.... *(2 marks)*

(b) Microwaves are used to transmit signals to the satellite. The microwaves have a wavelength of 0.6 metre (m) and travel through space at a speed of 300 000 000 metres per second (m/s).

(i) Write down the equation which links frequency, wavelength and wave speed.

.... *(1 mark)*

(ii) Calculate the frequency of the microwaves. Show clearly how you work out your answer and give the unit.

....

....

....

Frequency = ...

(3 marks)

11

marks

GRADE 'A' ANSWER

Daniel has correctly described both signals so gains both marks.

Daniel has made two correct points so gets two of the marks. He should have explained that the signals will need amplifying to travel over a long distance. He could also have said that noise in digital signals is low amplitude and treated as 'off'.

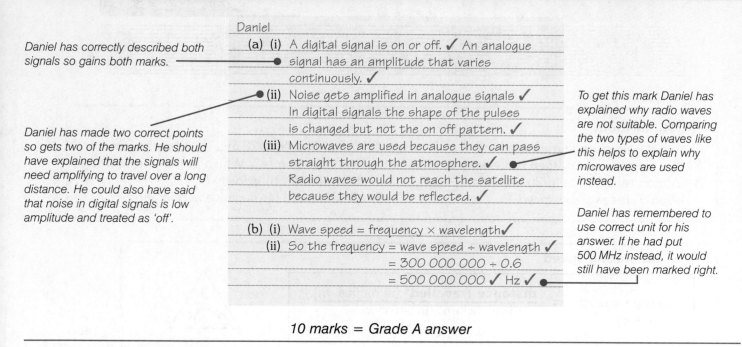

Daniel

(a) (i) A digital signal is on or off. ✓ An analogue signal has an amplitude that varies continuously. ✓

   (ii) Noise gets amplified in analogue signals ✓ In digital signals the shape of the pulses is changed but not the on off pattern. ✓

   (iii) Microwaves are used because they can pass straight through the atmosphere. ✓ Radio waves would not reach the satellite because they would be reflected. ✓

(b) (i) Wave speed = frequency × wavelength ✓

   (ii) So the frequency = wave speed ÷ wavelength ✓
       = 300 000 000 ÷ 0.6
       = 500 000 000 ✓ Hz ✓

To get this mark Daniel has explained why radio waves are not suitable. Comparing the two types of waves like this helps to explain why microwaves are used instead.

Daniel has remembered to use correct unit for his answer. If he had put 500 MHz instead, it would still have been marked right.

10 marks = Grade A answer

▶ **Improve your Grades   A up to A***

To get an A* grade it is important to give very full information in response to each question, especially in those questions that ask you to 'explain'.

GRADE 'C' ANSWER

Amy has correctly described a digital signal but she has not explained how it is different from an analogue signal, so she gets just 1 mark.

Amy has not really given any new information, she has just repeated the question so this does not get her any marks.

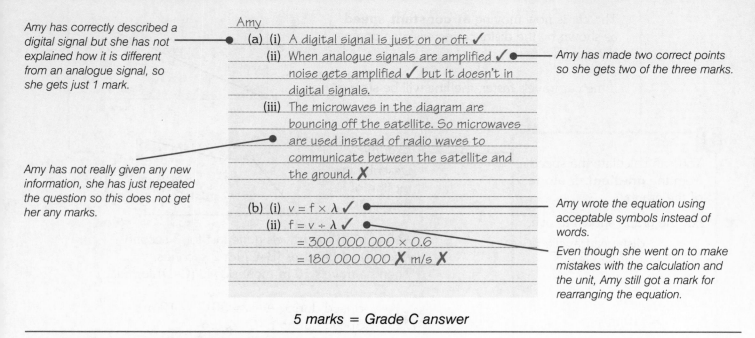

Amy

(a) (i) A digital signal is just on or off. ✓

   (ii) When analogue signals are amplified ✓ noise gets amplified ✓ but it doesn't in digital signals.

   (iii) The microwaves in the diagram are bouncing off the satellite. So microwaves are used instead of radio waves to communicate between the satellite and the ground. ✗

(b) (i) v = f × λ ✓

   (ii) f = v ÷ λ ✓
       = 300 000 000 × 0.6
       = 180 000 000 ✗ m/s ✗

Amy has made two correct points so she gets two of the three marks.

Amy wrote the equation using acceptable symbols instead of words.

Even though she went on to make mistakes with the calculation and the unit, Amy still got a mark for rearranging the equation.

5 marks = Grade C answer

▶ **Improve your Grades   C up to B**

Remember that you must give new information in your answers, not just put the question into different words.
If you are asked to give the difference between two things you must describe them both to show what the difference is.

VELOCITY and ACCELERATION

▶ ThinkAbout:

1. What unit is speed measured in?
2. If a car accelerates, then its velocity is . . . .
3. A man runs 100 m in 20 seconds.
   What is his average speed?

4. "A car travels at 20 m/s." "A bus travels North at 20 m/s." Which of these is referring to a) speed, b) velocity?
5. Give a word for negative acceleration.

▶ Calculating speed

$$\text{average speed (in m/s)} = \frac{\text{distance travelled (in metres, m)}}{\text{time taken (in seconds, s)}}$$

▶ Distance–time graphs for a car:

A horizontal line means that the car is **at rest**: (not moving, stationary).

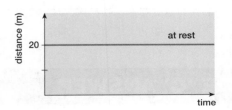

The car is now moving **at constant speed**, as shown by the distance increasing along a straight line:

If the car travels faster, the line will be steeper.

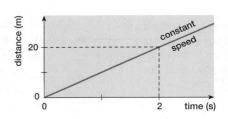

H

You can calculate the speed from the **gradient** or **slope** of the graph.

For the graph shown above,

$$\text{speed} = \frac{\text{distance travelled}}{\text{time taken}}$$

$$= \frac{20 \text{ m}}{2 \text{ s}}$$

$$= \underline{10 \text{ m/s}}$$

Example
Describe the motion of this cyclist:

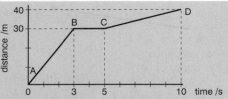

At first (A–B) he travels quite fast for 3 seconds.
After 30 m, he stops (B–C) for 2 seconds.
Then he travels 10 m more slowly (C–D) for 5 s.

H Speed during A–B = 30/3 = 10 m/s
Speed during B–C = zero
Speed during C–D = 10/5 = 2 m/s

Answers: 1. metres per second (metres/second, m/s) 2. changing 3. 5 m/s (100÷20) 4. a) the car, b) the bus, because it has a specific direction 5. deceleration/retardation

Velocity is speed in a particular direction.
For example, the pilot of a plane might be told to fly at 100 m/s due North. The direction is important.

If an object changes its velocity, it is **accelerating**.

▶ **Calculating acceleration**

$$\text{acceleration (in m/s}^2) = \frac{\text{change in velocity (m/s)}}{\text{time taken for the change (s)}}$$

▶ **Velocity–time graphs** for a car:

A horizontal line means that the car is travelling with a **constant velocity**.

In this graph the car starts off from rest (velocity = zero) and **accelerates uniformly** in a straight line.

In this graph the car accelerates more rapidly. The graph has a steeper *slope*.

The *area* under the graph line represents the distance travelled.

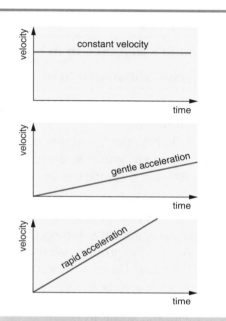

H

You can calculate the **acceleration** from the **gradient** or **slope** of the velocity–time graph.

In the graph shown at the right, the acceleration during P–Q

$$= \frac{\text{change in velocity}}{\text{time taken for change}}$$

$$= \frac{10 - 0 \ (\text{m/s})}{4 \ \text{s}}$$

$$= \underline{2.5 \ \text{m/s}^2}$$

Example
Describe the motion of this car.

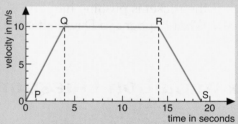

P–Q The car starts from rest and accelerates uniformly, until it reaches a velocity of 10 m/s after 4 s.

Q–R It stays at this speed for 10 seconds.

R–S The car decelerates, from 10 m/s to rest, in 5 s.

The **distance travelled** is shown by the **area under** the velocity–time graph.

In the graph shown at the right, the distance travelled during P–Q

$$= \text{area of triangle under P–Q}$$
$$= \tfrac{1}{2} \times \text{base} \times \text{height}$$
$$= \tfrac{1}{2} \times 4 \times 10$$
$$= \underline{20 \ \text{m}}$$

Take care:

- Make sure you look carefully in exam questions so you don't mix up distance–time and velocity–time graphs.

- In calculations make sure you show your working ... and include the correct units.

More in **Physics for You**, pages 122–126.

Velocity and acceleration

Homework Questions

1 What are the units for measuring velocity and acceleration? *(2 marks)*

2 Explain why velocity and speed are different quantities even though they can be measured in the same unit. *(2 marks)*

3 Rachel organises a 50 m race. Jamie runs and she rides her motor scooter. Another friend makes a video of the race. When they play the video, they collect this data:

Time in s	0	1	2	3	4	5	6	7	8
Jamie's distance in m	0	4	9	15	22	30	37	45	52
Rachel's distance in m	0	1	3	6	10	18	28	42	60

(a) Plot two distance–time graphs, one for Jamie and one for Rachel, using the same axes. *(2 marks)*
(b) Which is the independent variable in the data table? *(1 mark)*
(c) Use your graphs to decide who won the 50 m race, and the winning time. *(2 marks)*
(d) At what distance did the winner overtake? *(1 mark)*

4 Military pilots can use an ejector seat to throw them clear of the aircraft when they need to use their parachute in an emergency. David is testing the ejector seat in an aircraft parked on the ground. When the seat works, a rocket fires for 0.7 s and David's velocity increases evenly by 30 m/s.

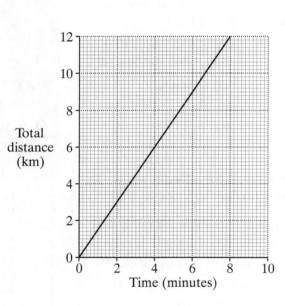

(a) Sketch a velocity–time graph to show how David moves. *(2 marks)*
H (b) Using the graph, or otherwise, calculate David's acceleration. *(2 marks)*
H (c) Use the graph to find how far David goes up in the air while the rocket is pushing him. *(2 marks)*
(d) What happens to David after the rocket stops working? *(2 marks)*

18 marks

Examination Questions

1 This is a distance–time graph for part of a train journey.
The train is travelling at a constant speed.

Total distance (km) vs Time (minutes) graph

Use the graph to find

(a) how far the train travels in 2 minutes. .... km

(b) how long it takes the train to travel a distance of 10 kilometres. .... minutes

(2 marks)

2 marks

2 The distance–time graph represents the motion of a car during a race.

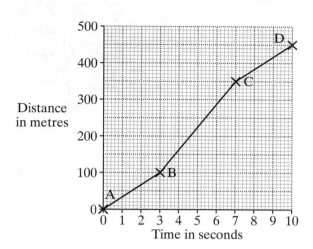

(a) Describe the motion of the car between point A and point D. You should not carry out any calculations.

To gain full marks in this question you should write your ideas in good English. Put them into a sensible order and use the correct scientific words.

....

....

....

....

....

....

(3 marks)

(b) Calculate the speed of the car between point B and point C. Show clearly how you get your answer.

....

....

....

....

....

gradient = ...

(3 marks)

6

marks

Answers on page 115

> ## ThinkAbout:

1. Cars and bicycles slow down because of the force of .... The brakes get ....
2. The force of friction always acts in the .... direction to the movement.
3. If the forces on an object cancel out they are said to be ....
   If they are not balanced then there is a .... force.

> ## Balanced forces

If the forces on an object are balanced (no resultant force) then:

- if it is at rest, it stays at rest,
- if it is moving, it keeps on moving at a constant speed in a straight line.

Object on a table
The forces are balanced

Car travelling at constant speed
The forces are balanced

> ## Unbalanced forces : resultant force

If the forces on an object do not cancel out, an unbalanced (resultant) force acts on the object, so that:

- a stationary object will start to move in the direction of the resultant force,
- an object already moving in the direction of the force will speed up (accelerate),
- an object moving in the opposite direction to the force will slow down (decelerate).

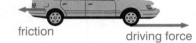

The car is accelerating
There is an unbalanced (resultant) force

The greater the resultant force, the greater the acceleration (or deceleration).
The bigger the mass of the object, the bigger the force needed to give it the same acceleration.

> ## Friction

A force of friction acts:

- when an object moves through air or water,
- when solid surfaces slide, or try to slide, across each other.

The objects heat up (and wear away).

> ## Gravity

Falling objects are accelerated downwards by gravity.
On Earth, the gravitational field strength is about 10 N/kg.
Weight is the pull of gravity on an object:

weight	**= mass**	**× gravitational field strength**
(newton, N)	(kilogram, kg)	(newton/kilogram, N/kg)

Example

What is the weight (on Earth) of a mass of 3 kg?

Weight = mass × gravitational field strength
= 3 kg × 10 N/kg
= <u>30 newtons</u>   (30 N)

Answers:

1. friction, hot   2. opposite
3. balanced, unbalanced (resultant)

Stopping distance

The total stopping distance of a car depends on:

- The 'thinking distance'. This depends on the driver's reaction time (which depends on tiredness, drugs and alcohol), and the speed.
- The 'braking distance'. This depends on the weather conditions (eg. wet/icy roads) and the vehicle (eg. worn brakes/tyres).

The greater the speed of the car, the more braking force, or distance, needed to stop it.

air resistance

weight

Terminal velocity

When an object falls through a fluid (gas or liquid), the faster it moves, the greater the force of friction.

When a body falls:
- at the start, it accelerates (due to the force of gravity (weight),
- frictional forces (eg. air resistance) increase ... until they balance the gravitational force,
- then the resultant force is zero, and the body falls at its 'terminal' velocity.

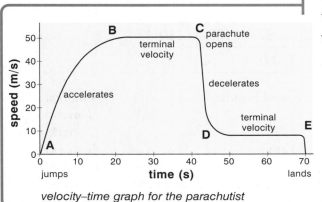

velocity–time graph for the parachutist

Force and acceleration

One newton (1 N) is the **force** needed to give a mass of one kilogram (1 kg) an acceleration of one metre per second squared (1 m/s²).

resultant force	**= mass**	**×**	**acceleration**
(newton, N)	(kilogram, kg)		(metre/second squared, m/s²)

Example

What is the force needed to give a mass of 3 kg an acceleration of 2 m/s²?

force = mass × acceleration

     = 3 kg × 2 m/s²

     = <u>6 newtons</u>   (6 N)

To see how to calculate an acceleration, see Topic 9.

Take care:

- Don't confuse mass (in kg) with weight (in N).

- Weight is a force (in N) and always acts downwards. Friction is a force (in N) and always acts backwards (opposing the movement).

- Remember an unbalanced force always produces an acceleration.

- In calculations, show your working and make sure that you use the right units.

More details in **Physics for You**, pages 65, 67–69, 82–89, 128, 130–131.

Forces

Homework Questions

1 Name the unit for measuring force. *(1 mark)*

2 What is the weight of a 25 kg bag of salt? (Gravitational field strength = 10 N/kg) *(1 mark)*

3 A sky-diver is falling at a terminal velocity of 55 m/s.
 (a) Explain why he is not accelerating. *(2 marks)*
 (b) Sketch a velocity–time graph to show what happens when he opens his parachute. *(1 mark)*
 (c) With his parachute open, the terminal velocity reduces to 5 m/s. Explain why it changed. *(2 marks)*

4 Lisa is testing the brakes on a new car. She measures the stopping distance from various speeds. These are her results:

Speed of car in km/h	30	50	60	80	100	110
Stopping distance in m	12	25	35	50	75	95

 (a) Plot a graph of Lisa's results and draw a curved line of best fit. *(3 marks)*
 (b) Which is the dependent variable? *(1 mark)*
 (c) Comment on the trend of the graph. *(1 mark)*
 (d) Estimate the stopping distance from a speed of 70 km/h. *(1 mark)*
 (e) Suggest how Lisa could improve the accuracy of her results. *(1 mark)*
 (f) List the factors, apart from speed, that affect the stopping distance of a car. *(3 marks)*

5 A space shuttle has a total mass of 100 000 kg. The pilot is manoeuvring the shuttle in orbit and she fires a rocket to provide a forward force of 27 000 N. The pilot's mass is 60 kg.
 (a) What is the acceleration of the shuttle? *(2 marks)*
 (b) The pilot feels a force on her while the rocket is firing. How big is the force? *(2 marks)*
 (c) At the same time, the pilot's body is pushing back on her chair. How big is this force? *(1 mark)*

_____
22
marks

Examination Question

A student carries out an experiment with a steel ball-bearing and a tube of thick oil.
The student releases the ball-bearing and it falls through the oil.

(a) Two forces **X** and **Y** act on the ball-bearing as it falls through the oil.
This is shown on the diagram below.

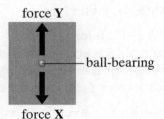

force **Y**

ball-bearing

force **X**

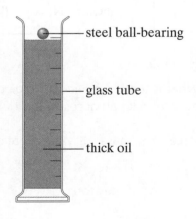

steel ball-bearing

glass tube

thick oil

Name force **X**. ....

Name force **Y**. ....
(2 marks)

(b) The graph shows how the speed of the ball-bearing changes as it falls through the oil.

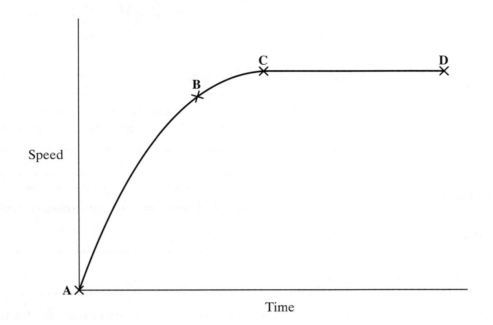

(i) What is happening to the speed of the ball-bearing between points **A** and **B**?

....

....

(1 mark)

Explain, in terms of forces **X** and **Y**, why this happens.

....

....

....

....

(1 mark)

(ii) What is happening to the speed of the ball bearing between points **C** and **D**?

....

....

....

(1 mark)

Explain, in terms of forces **X** and **Y**, why this happens.

....

....

....

....

....

(3 marks)

8 marks

Work and energy

▶ **ThinkAbout:**

1. A moving object has movement energy, also called . . . . energy.
2. When an object is lifted to a higher place, it is given . . . . potential . . . .

3. Energy can be . . . . from one form to . . . .
4. A falling object is . . . . energy from . . . . potential energy to . . . . energy.
5. A stretched catapult has . . . . potential . . . .

▶ **Work and energy**

When a force moves an object, energy is transferred and work is done. In fact:

> **work done   =   energy transferred**
> (joules, J)   (joules, J)

To calculate the work done (energy transferred):

> **work done   =   force applied   ×   distance moved in the direction of the force**
> (joules, J)   (newtons, N)   (metres, m)

Example 1

How much energy is transferred if a force of 2 N moves through a distance of 10 m?

work done = force × distance moved
          = 2 N × 10 m
          = 20 joules   (20 J)

∴ energy transferred = work done = 20 J

▶ **Gravitational potential energy**

When an object is lifted up, work is done against the force of gravity, its weight.

It follows (from the equations above) that:

> **change in gravitational potential energy   =   weight   ×   change in vertical height**
> (joules, J)   (newtons, N)   (metres, m)

Example 2

A man lifts up a brick of mass 5 kg from the floor to a shelf 2 metres high.
What is the change in gravitational potential energy of the brick?

Step 1 : Find the weight first (see Topic 10).
          weight = mass × gravitational field strength
                 = 5 kg × 10 N/kg   = 50 N

Step 2 :
change in gravitational potential energy = weight × change in vertical height

          = 50 N × 2 m   = 100 joules

Answers:

1. kinetic   2. gravitational, energy   3. transferred/transformed/changed, another   4. transferring, gravitational, kinetic   5. elastic, energy

▶ Potential energy

Gravitational potential energy is the energy *stored* in an object because of the height it has been lifted to, against the force of gravity.

Elastic potential energy is the energy stored in an elastic object, when work has been done on the object to change its shape (eg. a catapult).

▶ Kinetic energy (movement energy)

Kinetic energy can be transformed into other forms of energy, as shown in the table:

Example:	Kinetic energy is transformed to:
a car braking	heat in brakes + tyres
a wind turbine	electricity, heat, sound
roller-coaster car, going up a ramp	gravitational potential energy, heat
bullet fired into wood	heat
space-shuttle, re-entering atmosphere	heat

An object has more kinetic energy,
- if it has a bigger mass,
- if it travels at a higher speed.

H

The formula for kinetic energy is:

$$\text{kinetic energy} = \tfrac{1}{2} \times \text{mass} \times \text{speed}^2$$
$$\text{(joules, J)} \qquad \text{(kilogram, kg)} \quad \text{(m/s)}^2$$

Example 3

A car of mass 800 kg is travelling at 10 m/s.
How much kinetic energy has it got?

$$
\begin{aligned}
\text{kinetic energy} &= \tfrac{1}{2} \times \text{mass} \times \text{speed}^2 \\
&= \tfrac{1}{2} \times 800 \text{ kg} \times (10 \text{ m/s})^2 \\
&= \tfrac{1}{2} \times 800 \text{ kg} \times 100 \text{ m}^2/\text{s}^2 \\
&= \underline{40\,000 \text{ joules}} \quad (40 \text{ kJ})
\end{aligned}
$$

10 m/s

mass = 800 kg

braking force

Example 4

For the car in Example 3 above,
a) How much work must be done to stop it?
b) When the brakes are applied, it comes to rest in 8 m. What is the average force exerted by the brakes?

a) To stop the car,
work done = energy transferred = <u>40 000 joules</u>
This energy will be transferred to heat in the brakes/tyres.

b) From the opposite page:
$$
\begin{aligned}
\text{work done} &= \text{force} \times \text{distance moved} \\
40\,000 \text{ J} &= \text{force} \times 8 \text{ m} \\
\therefore \text{force} &= \underline{5000 \text{ newtons}}
\end{aligned}
$$

Take care:

- Remember work done against frictional forces is transferred mainly as heat.

- In calculations, always show your working ... so you may then get some marks even if the final answer is wrong.

More details in **Physics for You**, pages 97–99, 11, 109.

Work and energy

Homework Questions

1 What is the unit for measuring energy? *(1 mark)*

2 Ellen is riding her bicycle. It has squeaky brakes. List the energy transfers that happen when Ellen stops. *(3 marks)*

3 A bus and a motorbike are both travelling at 25 m/s. Explain why the bus has more kinetic energy. *(1 mark)*

4 Tahir is a weightlifter. He lifts a 1200 N weight through a distance of 2 m, holds it up and then drops it on to a mat.
(a) How much work does he do lifting the weight? *(2 marks)*
(b) Where is this energy when he holds the weight up? *(1 mark)*
(c) What happens to the energy when he drops the weight? *(1 mark)*

5 Tina weighs 500 N and she does 1250 J of work when she climbs the stairs.
What is the height of the staircase? *(2 marks)*

6 When John pushes a lawnmower 20 m, he does 800 J of work.
What force does he apply? *(2 marks)*

7 Dan is using a bow to shoot an arrow. He pulls on the bow and stores elastic potential energy in it. When Dan lets the arrow go, some of the stored energy is used to give the arrow its kinetic energy.
(a) Dan pulls the bow back 0.5 m. The average force is 110 N. How much work does he do? *(2 marks)*
(b) Why is the energy stored in the bow probably less than the amount you calculated? *(1 mark)*
(c) The arrow has a mass of 0.02 kg. When Dan shoots, it has 27 J of kinetic energy.
What is the velocity of the arrow? *(2 marks)*

H

18 marks

Examination Questions

1 'The Boat' is a theme park ride. 'The Boat' swings backwards and forwards. The diagrams show 'The Boat' at the top and bottom of its swing.

A   B   C

Sketch a graph to show how the gravitational potential energy of a child changes as 'The Boat' swings from **A** to **B** to **C**. The axes have been drawn for you.

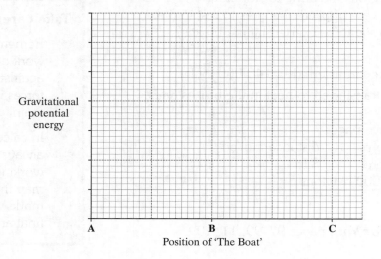

Gravitational potential energy

Position of 'The Boat'

(3 marks)

3 marks

54

2 (a) A chair lift carries two skiers, Greg and Jill, to the top of a ski slope.
Greg weighs 700 N and Jill weighs 500 N.

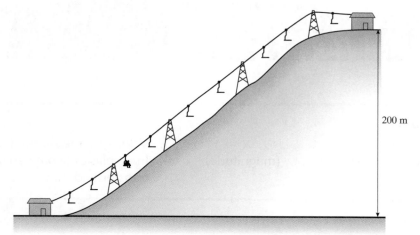

200 m

   (i) Write down the equation that links distance moved, force applied and work done.

   ....

   (1 mark)

   (ii) Calculate the work done to lift Greg and Jill through a vertical height of 200 m.
   Show clearly how you work out your answer and give the unit.

   ....

   ....

   ....

   work done = ...

   (3 marks)

(b) The chair takes 5 minutes to move from the bottom to the top of the ski slope.
Use the following equation to calculate the power required to lift Greg and Jill to the top
of the ski slope. Show clearly how you work out your answer.

$$\text{power} = \frac{\text{work done}}{\text{time taken}}$$

   ....

   ....

   power = ... watts   *(2 marks)*

(c) The chair lift is driven by an electric motor.

   (i) Why would the power output of the electric motor need to be larger than your
   answer to part (b)?

   ....

   ....

   (1 mark)

   (ii) Complete the following sentence.

   When the ski lift is working, ... energy supplied to the

   motor is usefully transferred as gravitational .... energy.

   (1 mark)

8 marks

12
AQA Topic P2.4

MOMENTUM MOMENTUM

ThinkAbout:

1. A force is measured in . . . .
2. A vector quantity has both . . . . (magnitude) and . . . .
3. Velocity is measured in . . . .
4. In a collision, some energy is always transformed into . . . .

Momentum

The momentum of an object depends only on its **mass** and **velocity**.
It is a vector quantity: it has both size (magnitude) and direction.

An object has more momentum,
- the greater its mass, and
- the greater its velocity.

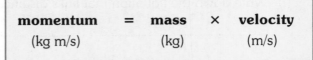

momentum	=	mass	×	velocity
(kg m/s)		(kg)		(m/s)

Example 1

A snooker ball has a mass of 0.2 kg and is travelling East at a velocity of 3 m/s. What is its momentum?

momentum = mass × velocity
= 0.2 kg × 3 m/s
= 0.6 kg m/s to the East

Changing momentum

When a force acts on a movable object, it changes the object's momentum:

H

force	=	**change in momentum** (kg m/s)
(N)		**time** that the force acts (s)

Example 2

A golf ball has a mass of 0.05 kg.
A golfer hits a still ball with a force of 500 N for 0.01 s.
What is then the velocity of the golf ball?

$$force = \frac{change\ in\ momentum}{time}$$

$$500\ N = \frac{0.05\ kg \times velocity}{0.01\ s}$$

so $velocity = \frac{500\ N \times 0.01\ s}{0.05\ kg} = \underline{100\ m/s}$

Answers: 1. newtons (N) 2. size, direction 3. metres per second (m/s) 4. heat

56

▶ Collisions (and explosions)

When 2 objects collide (eg. snooker balls),
they each exert a force on the other.
The momentum of one of them increases,
and the other decreases.

The total momentum stays the same.

We say the momentum is 'conserved'.
This means that:

total momentum before a collision	= **total momentum after the collision**

Example 3

In an accident, car A (mass 1500 kg)
travelling at 10 m/s bumps into the back of stationary car B
(mass 1000 kg). Car A is slowed to 4 m/s.
At what velocity v does car B jerk forward?

total momentum before = total momentum after

$(1500 \text{ kg} \times 10 \text{ m/s}) + 0 = (1500 \text{ kg} \times 4 \text{ m/s}) + (1000 \text{ kg} \times v)$

$15\,000 \text{ kg m/s} = 6000 \text{ kg m/s} + (1000 \text{ kg} \times v)$

so   velocity $v = \dfrac{9000 \text{ kg m/s}}{1000 \text{ kg}} = \underline{9 \text{ m/s}}$

The kinetic energy is usually
less after a collision.
It is not 'conserved'.
Some energy is transformed
to heat, sound, etc.

▶ Safety in car crashes

If you are travelling in a car you have momentum.
In any collision, to change your momentum,
a force is exerted on you for a length of time.
The *longer* the time, the *smaller* the force.

- Cars are designed to have **crumple zones**:
  These are parts of the car that fold up in a crash.
  This means that the collision time is *longer*,
  so the impact force is *less*.

- **Air-bags** inflate very quickly in a collision:
  Because of the air-bag, the change in momentum
  of the driver is spread out over a *longer* time,
  so the force is *less*.

- A **seat-belt** is designed to stretch in a collision,
  to make the deceleration time *longer*.

- A steering wheel is usually padded, so if you hit it,
  it spreads out the collision over a longer time.

- A cyclist's helmet is padded for the same reason.

- Similarly, if you jump down from a wall then you
  bend your knees to spread out the collision time.

More details in *Physics for You*, pages 136–138.

Take care:
- Do not confuse 'momentum'
  with 'moments' (see Topic 18).

- Remember that momentum is
  a vector quantity so it has a direction.

Momentum

Homework Questions

1 What is the unit for measuring momentum?   *(1 mark)*

2 Explain why momentum is a vector quantity.   *(2 marks)*

3 Explain how each of these safety features can reduce the force on a car passenger during an accident:
(a) a crumple zone,   (b) an air bag,   (c) a seat belt.   *(3 marks)*

4 When Dan's car turns a corner, its momentum changes even though its speed stays the same. How does this show that a force is needed to make a car turn a corner?   *(3 marks)*

5 When a star explodes (a supernova), matter flies away at high speed and in all directions, although there are no external forces. Explain how momentum can be conserved in a situation like this.   *(2 marks)*

6 Alison is at the ice rink, she is curling with 20 kg stones. She slides her stone along the ice and aims it to hit another one. Alison's stone is moving at 2.5 m/s when it hits a stationary stone.
After the collision, Alison's stone stops but the other stone moves away with a velocity of 2 m/s.

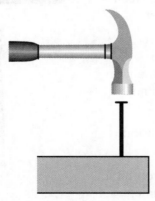

(a) Calculate the total momentum before and after the collision.   *(4 marks)*

(b) Suggest a reason why there is less total momentum after the collision.   *(1 mark)*

(c) Explain why the momentum of each stone changed as a result of the collision.   *(1 mark)*

[H] (d) Alison pushes steadily on another stone for 0.8 s and it gains 64 kg m/s of momentum.   ___19___
What was the unbalanced force on the stone?   *(2 marks)*   marks

Examination Question

(a) The diagram shows a hammer which is just about to drive a nail into a block of wood.

The mass of the hammer is 0.75 kg and its velocity, just before it hits the nail, is 15.0 m/s downward. After hitting the nail, the hammer remains in contact with it for 0.1 s. After this time both the hammer and the nail have stopped moving.

(i) Write down the equation, in words, which you need to use to calculate momentum.

.... *(1 mark)*

(ii) What is the momentum of the hammer just before it hits the nail?
Show how you work out your answer and give the units and direction.

....

....

....

....

Momentum = ...

(3 marks)

(iii) What is the change in momentum of the hammer during the time it is in contact with the nail?

.... *(1 mark)*

[H] (iv) Write down an equation which connects change in momentum, force and time.

.... *(1 mark)*

[H] (v) Calculate the force applied by the hammer to the nail.
Show how you work out your answer and give the unit.

....

....

....

....

Force = ...

(3 marks)

(b) A magazine article states that:

"Wearing a seat belt can save your life in a car crash."

Use your understanding of momentum to explain how this is correct.

....

....

....

....

....

....

....

....

(4 marks)

13 marks

Answers on page 116

Getting the Grades – Forces

Try this question, then compare your answer with the two examples opposite ▶

A car travelling along a straight road has to stop and wait at red traffic lights.
The graph shows how the velocity of the car changes after the traffic lights turn green.

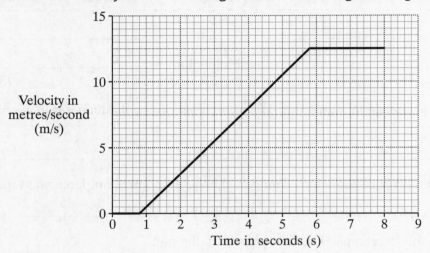

(a) Between the traffic lights changing to green and the car starting to move there is a time delay. This is called reaction time. Write down **one** factor that could affect the driver's reaction time.

.... *(1 mark)*

H (b) Calculate the distance the car travels while accelerating. Show clearly how you work out your answer.

....

....

Distance = ... metres

(3 marks)

H (c) Calculate the acceleration of the car. Show clearly how you work out your final answer and give the units.

....

....

....

Acceleration = ...

(4 marks)

(d) The mass of the car is 900 kg.

(i) Write down the equation that links acceleration, force and mass.

.... *(1 mark)*

(ii) Calculate the force used to accelerate the car. Show clearly how you work out your final answer.

....

....

Force = ...

(2 marks)

11

marks

GRADE 'A' ANSWER

Jack knows that being tired is one of the things that slows reaction time and so gets the first mark. He would have got the mark for other things too, such as the driver not concentrating or being under the influence of drugs or alcohol.

Jack knows that the area under a velocity–time graph gives the distance travelled. He reads the numbers correctly from the graph to find the area under the part of the graph where the car is accelerating. Unfortunately he makes a slip in the final part of the calculation. The correct answer is 31.25, but he loses only one mark as the rest of his working is correct.

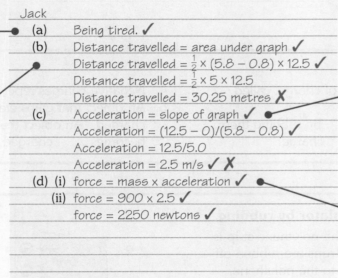

Jack
(a)   Being tired. ✓
(b)   Distance travelled = area under graph ✓
      Distance travelled = $\frac{1}{2}$ × (5.8 − 0.8) × 12.5 ✓
      Distance travelled = $\frac{1}{2}$ × 5 × 12.5
      Distance travelled = 30.25 metres ✗
(c)   Acceleration = slope of graph ✓
      Acceleration = (12.5 − 0)/(5.8 − 0.8) ✓
      Acceleration = 12.5/5.0
      Acceleration = 2.5 m/s ✓ ✗
(d) (i)   force = mass × acceleration ✓
    (ii)   force = 900 × 2.5 ✓
        force = 2250 newtons ✓

Jack knows that the slope of a velocity–time graph gives the acceleration. He reads the numbers from the graph and correctly works out the acceleration and so gains three marks. He loses the last mark because he forgets that the units of acceleration are m/s².

Jack gains all three marks for part (d) as he knows the equation and uses it to calculate the force correctly.

9 marks = Grade A answer

► **Improve your Grades**   **A up to A***
Take care with calculations. Maximise your marks by showing all your working and if you have time go back and check calculations for errors. Make sure that you know the units for all the quantities that you use in physics and can write the symbols for them correctly.

GRADE 'C' ANSWER

Sophie knows that driving too fast increases the stopping distance of a car, but this is not an answer to the question asked, so she does not get the mark.

Sophie knows that the area under a velocity–time graph gives the distance travelled. The question asks for the distance the car travels while accelerating, which is the area under the sloping part of the graph. Sophie also finds the distance travelled while the car is going at a constant speed so she does not get the last two marks.

Sophie
(a)   Driving too fast. ✗
(b)   Distance travelled = area under graph ✓
      Distance travelled = $\frac{1}{2}$ × (5.8 − 0.8) × 12.5
                  + (2 × 12.5) ✗
      Distance travelled = $\frac{1}{2}$ × 5 × 12.5 + 25
      Distance travelled = 56.25 metres ✗
(c)   Acceleration = slope of graph ✓
      Acceleration = (5.8 − 0.8)/(12.5 − 0) ✓
      Acceleration = 5.0/12.5
      Acceleration = 0.4 ✗ ✗
(d) (i)   newtons = kilograms × acceleration ✗
    (ii)   force= 900 × 0.4 ✓
        force = 360 newtons ✓

Sophie knows that the slope of a velocity–time graph gives the acceleration. She reads the numbers from the graph correctly and so gets the second mark. Unfortunately Sophie puts the calculation upside down and forgets to give a unit so she loses the last two marks.

Sophie has used some units in her equation, instead of the quantities given in the question, so she does not get the mark.

Sophie's value for acceleration is wrong, but she uses it correctly with the mass to calculate the force and so gains both marks.

5 marks = Grade C answer

► **Improve your Grades**   **C up to B**
Always read the question carefully and make sure you answer what is asked. If you a taking values from graphs take care that you read the numbers correctly and that you are using the correct region on the graph. Know how to find slopes of graphs and areas under graphs. Learn word equations carefully and do not mix up quantities and units.

▷ **ThinkAbout:**

1. There are two kinds of charge, called positive and . . . .
2. Insulators can be . . . . by rubbing them.
3. Electrons have a . . . . charge.

4. Negative charges repel other . . . . charges.
5. An object that gains electrons becomes . . . . charged. An object that loses electrons becomes . . . . charged.

▷ **Charging an insulator by rubbing**

In the diagram, when the polythene strip is rubbed with wool, electrons are rubbed off the wool and move on to the polythene.

Electrons are negative.
Only the electrons move.

The polythene now has more electrons, so it is negative.

The wool is short of electrons, so it is positive.

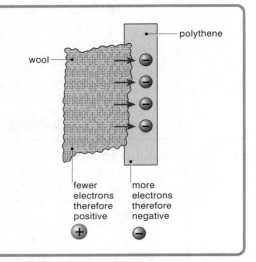

▷ **Forces between charges**

Two charged objects have an electric force between them:

> Like charges repel.
> Unlike charges attract.

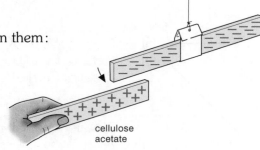

▷ **Conduction of electricity**

Electrons can flow through a solid conductor (eg. a copper wire).
Electrons can flow easily through metals.
Metals are good conductors, because they have free electrons.

The *rate* of flow of electric charge is called the current.

See also Topic 16: $\text{current (in amps)} = \dfrac{\text{charge (in coulombs)}}{\text{time (in seconds)}}$

▷ Dangers of electrostatics

The more charge put on an object, the higher the voltage (potential difference) between the object and earth.
If the potential difference is very high, then a **spark** can jump between the object and any earthed conductor.
This can be dangerous.

▷ Preventing fires and explosions

A liquid (or a powder) flowing through a pipe can become charged by rubbing. This can be dangerous if it causes a spark and the substance is inflammable.
For this reason, whenever an aeroplane is being re-fuelled by a tanker, they are always connected together by a copper wire.

You may feel a shock if you touch a metal door handle after walking on a nylon carpet, or riding on a car seat.

▷ Using electrostatics

An **electrostatic precipitator** can be used to remove smoke particles in a chimney:

In the diagram, the smoke particles pick up a positive charge as they pass by the grid (+).

They are then repelled by the positive grid and attracted to the (negative) plates.
The particles stick there, until they are knocked off and collected.

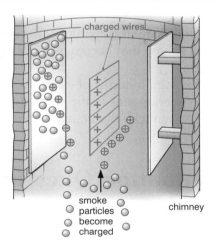

In a **photocopier**, a metal drum is charged up.
An image of the page to be copied is projected on to the drum. Where the light shines on the drum the charges leak away, leaving a pattern of the page:

Black ink powder is attracted to these charged parts of the drum.

This ink is then transferred to a sheet of paper.
The paper is heated so that the ink powder melts and sticks to the paper.

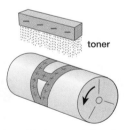

Powdered ink (toner) is attracted to the charged parts of the drum, before being transferred to paper

More details in **Physics for You**, pages 241–247, 315.

Take care:

- Make sure you know about one use and one danger of electrostatics.

- Remember that only negative charges (electrons) can move in wires.

Static electricity

Homework Questions

1 Describe the force between two positive charges. *(1 mark)*

2 Describe the force between two negative charges. *(1 mark)*

3 What is the name for the rate of flow of charge? *(1 mark)*

4 State **two** dangers of static electricity. *(2 marks)*

5 Lee has some new memory chips for his computer. He knows that integrated circuits like computer memory can be damaged by electrostatic discharge. Before he opens the computer to fit the new memory, Lee uses a special conducting cable to connect himself to the earthed metal case of the computer.
(a) Suggest why Lee might have electrostatic charge. *(2 marks)*
(b) Explain how any charge on Lee will be discharged. *(2 marks)*

6 Explain carefully, in terms of electrons, how a glass rod can be positively charged by rubbing it with a dry cloth. *(3 marks)*

7 Explain how electrostatic forces are used in a photocopier to transfer ink powder to the drum (which later puts it on the paper). *(4 marks)*

8 A Van de Graaff generator is designed to produce electrostatic charge. It has an insulated metal sphere that becomes positively charged. More charge is added steadily to the metal sphere.
(a) Explain, in terms of electrons, how positive charge is added to the sphere. *(2 marks)*
(b) What happens to the voltage of the metal sphere as its charge increases? *(1 mark)*
(c) Explain why the voltage of the metal sphere might cause sparking. *(1 mark)*

$\overline{}$
20
marks

Examination Questions

1 One method of painting a car uses electrostatics. A paint spray produces paint droplets, all of which are given a positive charge. The car body is given a negative charge.

positively charged paint droplets

negatively charged car body

(a) Explain why it is important to give all of the paint droplets a positive charge.

....

.... *(2 marks)*

(b) Explain why it is important to give the car body a negative charge.

....

$\overline{}$
4

.... *(2 marks)* marks

2 (a) Burning fuels produce smoke particles and waste gases. An electrostatic smoke precipitator can remove the smoke particles from the waste gases.

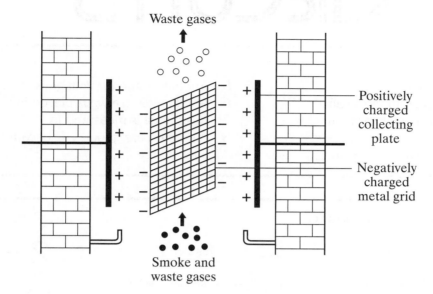

The following sentences **A** to **E** describe how this electrostatic smoke precipitator works. The sentences are in the wrong order.

A The smoke particles stick to the positively charged collecting plates.

B The smoke particles are given a negative charge.

C The waste gases and smoke pass through a negatively charged metal grid.

D The collecting plates are knocked so the smoke particles fall and can be taken away.

E The smoke particles are repelled from the grid and attracted to the positively charged collecting plates.

Arrange the sentences in the right order. Start with sentence **C**.

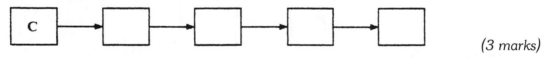

(3 marks)

(b) The underground storage tanks at petrol stations are filled from tankers. A static electric charge can build up on the tanker as the petrol flows through the pipe to the storage tank. This could be dangerous.

Why is the static electric charge dangerous and what should be done to stop the charge building up?

....

(2 marks)

CIRCUITS

▷ ThinkAbout:

1. A current is a flow of . . . .
2. Current is measured in units called . . . .
3. If the same current goes through 2 components, they are in . . . .
4. An ammeter is always placed in . . . .
5. Another name for voltage is . . . .
6. A voltmeter is always placed in . . . .
7. Resistance is measured in . . . .
8. All metals are good . . . . because they have a lot of free . . . .

▷ Circuit symbols to remember:

switch (open)	resistor	lamp (or)
switch (closed)	variable resistor	
cell	fuse	
battery	thermistor	ammeter (A)
diode	LDR	voltmeter (V)

▷ Resistors in series

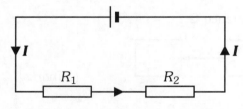

- The same current I goes through all the components.

- The potential difference across the cell is shared between the 2 resistors.

- The larger resistance has the larger p.d. across it.

- In the diagram above, total resistance, $R = R_1 + R_2$

▷ Resistors in parallel

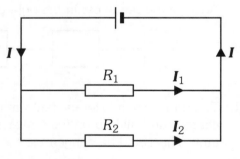

- The p.d. across R_1 is equal to the p.d. across R_2 (and equal to the p.d. of the cell).

- The current I from the cell is shared between the 2 branches.

- The larger resistance has the smaller current through it.

- In the diagram above, total current, $I = I_1 + I_2$

Answers:

1. electrons   2. amperes (amps)   3. series   4. series   5. potential difference (p.d.)   6. parallel   7. ohms (Ω)   8. conductors, electrons

66

▷ Current : voltage graphs

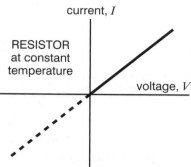

RESISTOR at constant temperature

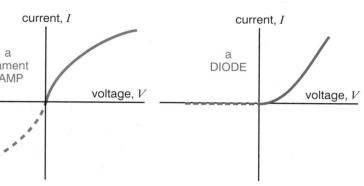

a filament LAMP

a DIODE

If a resistor is kept at constant temperature, the **current I** through it is proportional to the **voltage V** across the resistor.

When a current flows through the lamp, it gets hotter, and so its resistance increases ... and so the curve bends as shown.

In a diode, the current can flow one way only. It has a very high resistance in the reverse direction.

The dotted part of the graph shows what happens when you reverse the voltage.

LDR, Light-Dependent Resistor

As more light shines on this resistor, its resistance decreases, so that more current flows.

Thermistor

When this resistor gets hotter, its resistance decreases, so that more current flows.

▷ Potential difference V, current I, and resistance R

potential difference, V = **current, I** × **resistance, R**
(in volts, V)　　　　　　(in amps, A)　　　(in ohms, Ω)

$$V = I \times R$$

Example

What is the current in this circuit?

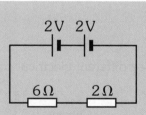

2V 2V

6Ω   2Ω

Total p.d. $= 2V + 2V = 4\ V$

Total resistance $= 6\,\Omega + 2\,\Omega = 8\,\Omega$

$$V = I \times R$$
$$4V = I \times 8\,\Omega$$
so $I = \tfrac{1}{2}$ amp $= \underline{0.5\ A}$

Take care:

- Make sure you are clear about the differences between series and parallel circuits.

- Ammeters are always in series, voltmeters always in parallel.

- Make sure you include units (volts, amps or ohms) in your calculations.

- Learn all the circuit symbols.

More details in **Physics for You**, pages 248–259, 318.

Circuits

Homework Questions

1 Name the unit for resistance. *(1 mark)*

2 Draw the circuit symbols for a fuse, a resistor and a thermistor. *(3 marks)*

3 Sunil puts three new $1\frac{1}{2}$ V batteries into his torch.
(a) What voltage should the three batteries provide together? *(1 mark)*
(b) If one of the batteries is put in the wrong way round, how will it affect the way the torch works? *(2 marks)*

4 Explain, in terms of resistance, why current only flows easily in one direction in a diode. *(2 marks)*

5 A LDR is connected in series with a lamp and a battery. The lamp lights. Explain what will happen if the lamp is moved closer to the LDR, allowing more light to shine on it. *(3 marks)*

6 Ayesha measures the resistance of a filament lamp at different voltages. These are her results:

Voltage in V	4.8	6.0	7.2	8.4	9.6	10.8	12.0	13.2	14.4
Resistance in Ω	6.6	7.4	8.1	8.8	9.4	9.9	10.3	10.6	10.9

(a) Plot a graph of Ayesha's results. *(3 marks)*
(b) Suggest a reason for the change in the resistance of the lamp. *(1 mark)*
(c) Calculate the current in the lamp when the voltage is 12.0 V. *(2 marks)*

7 Luke sets up this circuit. The p.d. across component **A** is 1 V and the current in it is 0.002 A.
(a) What is the total resistance of component **A**?
(b) What is the current in component **B**?
(c) Luke warms component **A**.
Explain what happens to:
(i) the resistance of component **A**,
(i) the current in component **B**, and
(i) the voltage across component **B**. *(6 marks)*

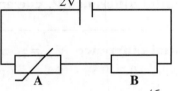

24 marks

Examination Questions

1 The diagram shows the voltage–current graphs for three different electrical components.

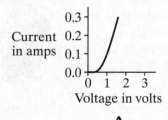

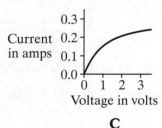

Which **one** of the components, **A**, **B** or **C**, could be a 3-volt filament lamp?
Explain the reason for your choice.

....

....

.... 3

(3 marks) marks

2 A set of Christmas tree lights is made from twenty identical lamps connected in series.

(a) Each lamp is designed to take a current of 0.25 A. The set plugs directly into the 230 V mains electricity supply.

   (i) Write down the equation that links current, potential difference and resistance.

....

(1 mark)

  (ii) Calculate the resistance of **one** of the lamps. Show clearly how you work out your final answer and give the unit.

....

....

....

....

....

Resistance = ...

(4 marks)

 (iii) What is the total resistance of the set of lights?

....

Total resistance = ...

(1 mark)

(b) How does the resistance of a filament lamp change as the temperature of the filament changes?

....

(1 mark)

$\dfrac{7}{\text{marks}}$

Answers on page 116

Mains electricity

▶ ThinkAbout:

1. Mains electricity in the UK is supplied at a . . . . voltage.
   If not used carefully, it can be . . . .
2. In a fuse, the wire should . . . . if the current is too . . . .

3. A mains plug has . . . . pins.
   Some parts of the plug are made of plastic, because plastic is a good . . . .
   Some parts are made of brass, because brass is a good . . . .

▶ The 3-pin plug

When connecting the wires you must ensure that:

- the blue wire is connected to the neutral terminal,
- the brown wire is connected to the live terminal,
- the green/yellow wire is connected to the earth terminal,
- the cable should be held firmly in the cable-grip,
- a *fuse* of the correct value (rating) must be fitted.

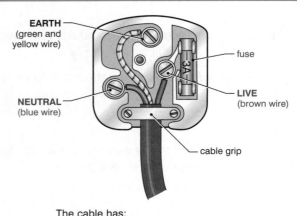

The cable has:
- a plastic cover (plastic is an insulator),
- copper wires inside (good conductor).

▶ The earth wire – for safety

In the UK, the mains supply is 230 V and can easily kill you.
Appliances with metal cases need to be *earthed*.
The case is connected to the earth pin (by the green/yellow wire).
If a fault connects the case to the live wire, then a large current flows to earth and melts the fuse.

The **fuse**:

- must be in the live wire, so the appliance becomes disconnected,
- should have a value (rating) higher than (but as close as possible to) the normal working current,
- can be replaced by a circuit-breaker.

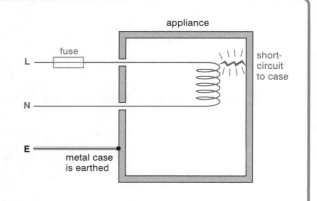

▷ Alternating current (a.c.)

An alternating current (a.c.) is constantly changing direction, to and fro:

Compare this with direct current (d.c.) from a battery.

Mains electricity is an a.c. supply. In the UK it has a frequency of 50 hertz (50 Hz), so each cycle lasts for 1/50 second, as shown:

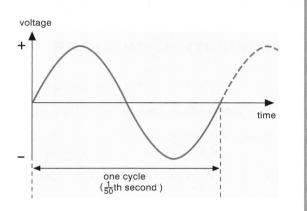

voltage

time

one cycle
($\frac{1}{50}$th second)

H

The mains supply in the UK is 230 volts.

The **live** terminal of the mains supply alternates between a positive and a negative voltage with respect to the neutral terminal, as shown above.

The **neutral** terminal stays at a voltage close to zero with respect to earth.

Take care:

Make sure you know how to wire a 3-pin mains plug.

▷ Measuring with an oscilloscope

An oscilloscope (CRO) displays a waveform.

It can be used to measure:
- the voltage (p.d.) of d.c. or a.c. supplies,
- the frequency of an a.c. supply.

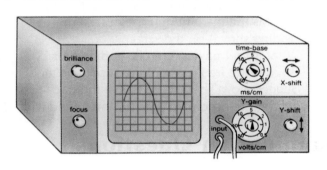

Example 1

A **d.c.** supply is connected to an oscilloscope:

before   *after*

Suppose the Y-sensitivity is 4 V/cm

You can see that the spot has moved up 2 squares = 2 cm

So:
the voltage = 2 cm × 4 V/cm
= <u>8 V</u>

Example 2

An a.c. supply is connected to a CRO with the time-base on:

before   *after*

Suppose the Y-sensitivity is 4 V/cm

The spot has moved up 2 cm

So:
Peak voltage = 2 cm × 4 V/cm
= <u>8 V</u>

Example 3 **H**

An a.c. supply is connected to an oscilloscope with the time-base on:

before   *after*

X-time-base = 0.01 second/cm

One complete oscillation = 4 cm (horizontally)

So:
Time period = 4 cm × 0.01 s/cm
= <u>0.04 second</u>

Frequency = $\frac{1}{\text{time}}$ = $\frac{1}{0.04}$ = <u>25 Hz</u>

More details in **Physics for You**, pages 268–270, 299, 311.

Mains electricity

Homework Questions

1 Name the wires that are connected in a 3-pin plug. *(3 marks)*

2 State **three** safety features of a 3-pin plug. *(3 marks)*

3 Draw a diagram to show the structure of a mains cable. Colour and label the wires. *(3 marks)*

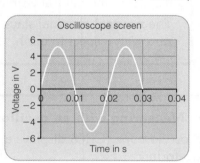

4 Explain what is meant by the term 'direct current.' *(2 marks)*

5 Explain how a fuse protects a circuit against excess current. *(2 marks)*

6 The metal case of a toaster is connected to the earth wire. Explain why this could help to protect both the appliance and the user if the toaster has a wiring fault. *(3 marks)*

H 7 In a mains supply, what is the potential difference between:
(a) the neutral wire and the live wire, and
(b) the neutral wire and the earth wire? *(3 marks)*

8 Theo is using an oscilloscope to test a power supply. The time and voltage axes are both shown on the screen.
(a) What type of current is the power supply providing? *(1 mark)*
(b) Explain how Theo could make the oscilloscope trace brighter and then move it to the right. *(2 marks)*
(c) What is the maximum positive voltage reading shown on the screen? *(1 mark)*
(d) What is the maximum voltage difference? *(1 mark)*
H (e) What is the frequency of the supply voltage? *(3 marks)*
(f) Suggest how Theo could adjust the trace to get a more accurate value for the frequency. *(2 marks)*

29 marks

Examination Questions

1 The diagram shows an iron connected to an electrical socket by a cable and 3-pin plug.

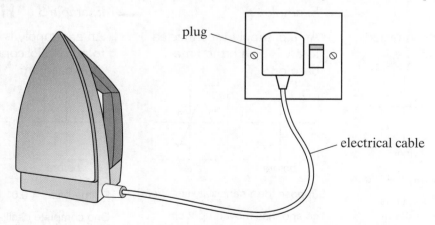

plug

electrical cable

(a) Describe the structure of the electrical cable which connects the plug to the iron.

....

....

....

.... *(3 marks)*

(b) The diagram shows a 3-pin electrical plug.

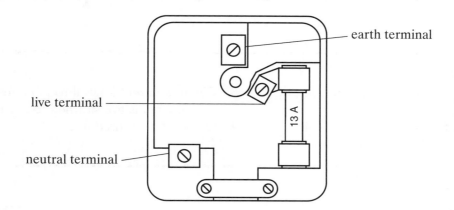

live terminal

neutral terminal

earth terminal

13 A

Describe how the cable should be connected to the terminals of the plug.

....

....

....

....

(2 marks)

5 marks

2 The drawings show an electric kettle and an electric hair-dryer.

kettle with metal case   hair-dryer with plastic case

(a) Why does the kettle need to be earthed, but not the hair-dryer?

....

....

(1 mark)

(b) Explain how earthing the kettle protects the user.

....

....

....

....

....

....

(4 marks)

5 marks

Answers on page 117

Power in electrical appliances

> **ThinkAbout:**
>
> 1. An electric current is measured in . . . . by using an . . . .
> 2. A potential difference (p.d. or . . . .) is measured in . . . . by using a . . . .
> 3. When a current flows through a resistor, ... energy is transformed to . . . . energy.
> 4. Energy is measured in . . . .
>   1 kJ = ...

▷ **Electrical appliances**

Electrical appliances are used to transform electrical energy to some other useful form of energy.

This energy may be light, sound, kinetic energy and heat. See the examples in Topic 3 (page 16).

▷ **Power**

Power is a measure of how fast the energy is transformed.
The greater the power, the more energy is transformed in a given time.

$$\textbf{power}\ \text{(in watts, W)}\ =\ \frac{\textbf{energy transformed}\ \text{(in joules, J)}}{\textbf{time taken}\ \text{(in seconds, s)}}$$

1 watt is the rate of transforming 1 joule in 1 second.

You can also calculate the power from the work done, because energy transferred = work done, see Topic 11.

Example 1

An MP3 player transfers 4 J of electrical energy (from the battery) to sound energy in 10 seconds. What is the power, in watts?

$$\text{power} = \frac{\text{energy transformed}}{\text{time taken}}$$

$$= \frac{4}{10}$$

$$= \underline{0.4\ \text{watts}} \quad (0.4\ \text{W})$$

Example 2

A 100 W lamp is switched on for 2 hours. How much energy is transferred to the room?

$$\text{power} = \frac{\text{energy transformed}}{\text{time taken}}$$

$$100\ \text{W} = \frac{\text{energy transformed}}{2\ \times\ 60\ \times\ 60\ \text{seconds}}$$

$$\therefore \text{energy transformed} = 100\ \text{W} \times 2 \times 60 \times 60\ \text{s}$$

$$= \underline{720\ 000\ \text{joules}} \quad (= 720\ \text{kJ})$$

More details in
Physics for You,
pages 110–111.

▷ Heating a resistor

An electric current is a flow of charge.
When the charge flows through a resistor, electrical energy is transferred as heat (eg. in a lamp).

The rate of energy transfer (the power) is given by:

power = **current** × **potential difference**	
(watt, W) (ampere, A) (volt, V)	

Example 3

In the circuit shown, what is the power of the lamp?

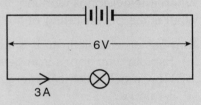

6 V

3 A

$$\text{power} = \text{current} \times \text{p.d.}$$
$$= 3\,A \times 6\,V$$
$$= \underline{18\,W} \quad (18 \text{ joules/s})$$

Example 4

Here is the plate at the back of a vacuum cleaner. What fuse is needed for it?

Model 5350
230 V ~50 Hz 500 W
BEAB approved

$$\text{power} = \text{current} \times \text{p.d.}$$
$$500\,W = \text{current} \times 230\,V$$
$$\therefore \text{current} = \frac{500\,W}{230\,V} = 2.2\,A$$

The next size of fuse is 3 amps.
So a <u>3 A fuse</u> should be fitted.

H

If the voltage (p.d.) is higher and the charge is bigger, then more energy is transformed, because:

energy transformed =	**p.d.** ×	**charge**
(joule, J)	(volt, V)	(coulomb, C)

The amount of charge is given by:

charge =	**current** ×	**time**
(coulomb, C)	(ampere, A)	(seconds, s)

More details in
Physics for You,
pages 266–267,
260–261.

Example 5   **H**

In the circuit shown above,
a) how much charge flows in 10 seconds?
b) how much energy is transformed during this time?

a) $\quad \text{charge} = \text{current} \times \text{time}$
$$= 3\,A \times 10\,s$$
$$= \underline{30 \text{ coulomb}} \quad (30\,C)$$

b) $\quad \text{energy transformed} = \text{p.d.} \times \text{charge}$
$$= 6\,V \times 30\,C$$
$$= \underline{180\,J}$$

Note : see the answer to Example 3 above.
18 J/s for 10 seconds gives the same answer by a different route.

Take care:

You may find it helps to convert each of these formulas into a formula triangle, like:

$$\frac{P}{I \times V}$$

Make sure you always put the right units on your answer.

Power in electrical appliances

Homework Questions

1 Name the unit for electric power.   *(1 mark)*

2 Explain the meaning of the term 'electric current.'   *(2 marks)*

3 When a television is working, the mains current is 0.4 A. The mains voltage is 230 V.
   What is the power rating of the television?   *(2 marks)*

4 Tom has an electric iron. It is labelled 230 V 50 Hz 1200 W.
   (a) Explain why Tom's iron gets hot when it is switched on.   *(1 mark)*
   (b) How much electrical energy does the iron use when Tom switches it on for
       1 minute?   *(2 marks)*
   (c) Calculate the current in the iron when it is working.   *(2 marks)*
   (d) Suggest an appropriate value for the fuse in the mains plug of Tom's iron.
       Explain your answer.   *(1 mark)*

5 A torch bulb is marked 2.2 V 250 mA. (*Hint:* 250 mA is the same as 0.25 A.)
   The bulb is connected to a 2.2 V supply and it is bright.
   (a) How much electrical energy is transferred in the bulb in 1 second?   *(2 marks)*
   H (b) When the bulb is connected instead to a 1.5 V battery it is dimmer.
       Explain why.   *(2 marks)*

6 A yoghurt making machine uses a 10 W heater to keep the milk warm while it is
   turning into yoghurt. The mains voltage is 230 V. Calculate:
   (a) the current in the heater when it is working,
   H (b) the amount of energy transferred when 1 C of charge passes through the heater,   21
   H (c) the amount of charge that passes through the heater in 1 hour.   *(6 marks)* marks

Examination Questions

1 The information plate on a hair-dryer is shown.

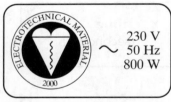

230 V
50 Hz
800 W

(a) What is the power rating of the hair-dryer?

   .... *(1 mark)*

(b) (i) Write down the equation which links *current*, *power* and *voltage*.

   .... *(1 mark)*

   (ii) Calculate the current in amperes, when the hair-dryer is being used.
        Show clearly how you work out your answer.

   ....

   ....

                        Current = ... amperes
                                                                                 (2 marks)

(iii) Which **one** of the following fuses, 3 A, 5 A or 13 A, should you use with this hair-dryer?

....

(1 mark)

5

marks

2 The diagram shows a circuit which can be used to silver-plate a nickel spoon.

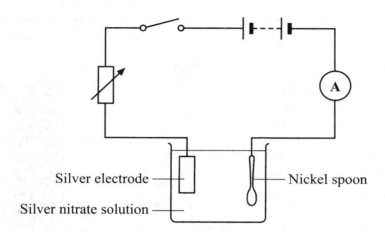

Silver electrode

Silver nitrate solution

Nickel spoon

(a) Silver nitrate solution contains silver ions. When the switch is closed, the silver ions move towards the spoon. Are the silver ions negatively or positively charged?
Give a reason for your answer.

....

....

(2 marks)

H (b) With the switch closed, the ammeter reads 0.5 A. In 30 minutes, 1.0 g of silver is deposited on the spoon.

(i)   Write down the equation which links charge, current and time.

....

(1 mark)

(ii) Calculate the charge which flows in 30 minutes. Show clearly how you get your final answer and give the units.

....

....

Charge = ...

(2 marks)

5

marks

Answers on page 117

Radioactive decay; Fission & fusion

▶ **ThinkAbout:**

1. Atoms have a small central . . . . , made up of protons and . . . . , around which there are . . . .

2. . . . . are positive, ... are negative, while neutrons have no . . . .

3. . . . . are much lighter than . . . . or . . . .

▶ **Atomic structure** **H**

At one time, scientists believed in a 'plum-pudding' model of the atom. They believed that the negative electrons were stuck in a positive blob of matter.

Then Rutherford and Marsden fired alpha-particles at gold foil, which scattered them, as shown:

Rutherford showed that this means an atom has a tiny heavy positive nucleus.

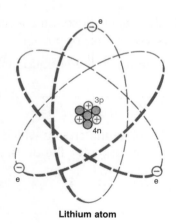

gold nucleus

α-particles

The paths of the positive alpha-particles show that they are being repelled by the positive nuclei of the atoms

We now know the nucleus is made of protons (+) and neutrons, around which are the electrons (–). In a neutral atom, the number of electrons equals the number of protons. Atoms can gain or lose electrons to become charged particles called **ions**.

	mass	charge
proton	1	+1
neutron	1	0
electron	negligible	–1

▶ **Proton number, mass number**

All atoms of an element have the same number of protons. All atoms of lithium (Li) have 3, as shown:

Different elements have different numbers of protons. The number of protons in an atom is called its **atomic number** (or proton number).

3p
4n

e

e   e

Lithium atom

Atoms of the same element can have different numbers of neutrons. These are **isotopes**. The isotope of lithium shown here has 4 neutrons. Other isotopes of lithium can have 3 or 5 neutrons.

The total number of protons + neutrons in an atom is called its **mass number** (or nucleon number).

number of nucleons (mass number)
(protons + neutrons)

$$^{7}_{3}\text{Li}$$

number of protons (atomic number)

▶ Radioactive decay

Radioactivity occurs as a result of changes in the nuclei of atoms.
A radioactive isotope is an atom with an unstable nucleus.
When it splits up (decays):

● it emits radiation (α, β, and/or γ),

● a different atom is formed, with a different number of protons:

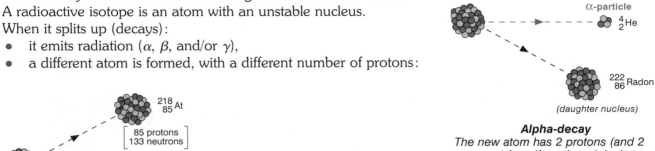

$^{226}_{88}$ Radium
(parent nucleus)

α-particle
$^4_2$He

$^{222}_{86}$ Radon

(daughter nucleus)

Alpha-decay
*The new atom has 2 protons (and 2 neutrons) **less than** the original atom. It is a different element.*

$^{218}_{85}$ At

$\begin{bmatrix} 85 \text{ protons} \\ 133 \text{ neutrons} \end{bmatrix}$

β-particle
$^{\ 0}_{-1}$ e

$^{218}_{84}$ Po

$\begin{bmatrix} 84 \text{ protons} \\ 134 \text{ neutrons} \end{bmatrix}$

Beta-decay
*A neutron changes into a proton and an electron (which is emitted as a β-particle). The new atom has 1 proton **more than** the original atom. It is a different element.*

▶ Background radiation

This comes from both natural and artificial (man-made) sources, as shown:

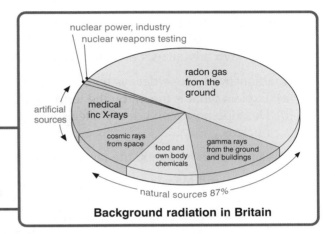

nuclear power, industry
nuclear weapons testing

radon gas
from the
ground

artificial
sources

medical
inc X-rays

cosmic rays
from space

food and
own body
chemicals

gamma rays
from the ground
and buildings

natural sources 87%

Background radiation in Britain

▶ Nuclear fission

Nuclear fission is used to provide energy in nuclear reactors (eg. in nuclear power stations).

When an atom with a large nucleus (like uranium-235 or plutonium-239) is bombarded with a neutron:

● the nucleus may split ('fission') into two smaller nuclei,

● 2 or 3 neutrons are released, which can cause a **chain reaction** as shown:

● energy is released.

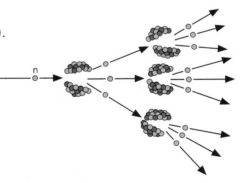

n

▶ Nuclear fusion

Nuclear fusion is the joining together of 2 small atomic nuclei to form a larger one.
This is how a star (like the Sun) releases energy from its hydrogen fuel.

2 hydrogen nuclei $\xrightarrow{\text{nuclear fusion}}$ helium nucleus + energy

Take care:

● Be clear about the differences between alpha decay and beta decay.

● Make sure you can distinguish fission from fusion.

More in **Physics for You**, pages 342–343, 345, 348–350, 372, 156.

Radioactive decay; Fission and fusion

Homework Questions

1 What is the name for the charged particles formed when atoms lose electrons? *(1 mark)*

2 An electron, a proton and a neutron are all particles.
   (a) Write down the relative mass of each. *(3 marks)*
   (b) State the charge of each particle. *(3 marks)*

3 Explain what is meant by the term 'nuclear fission.' *(2 marks)*

4 Name a fissionable substance used in nuclear reactors. *(1 mark)*

5 Describe the stages of the chain reaction that occurs in nuclear reactors.
   (You may draw a diagram to show this if you prefer.) *(5 marks)*

6 Some people think that providing energy from nuclear reactors might be a bad idea.
   Other people disagree and are in favour of nuclear energy.
   Suggest **two** advantages and **two** disadvantages of using nuclear reactors. *(4 marks)*

7 A radioactive isotope decays by emitting alpha particles.
   (a) Explain what is meant by the term 'isotope'. *(2 marks)*
   (b) Describe how alpha decay affects the number of protons and neutrons in the
      nucleus. *(2 marks)*

8 Explain what is meant by the term 'nuclear fusion.' *(2 marks)*

H 9 Rutherford and Marsden aimed alpha particles at the atoms in a very thin sheet of gold.
   They recorded how the alpha particles were scattered after hitting the gold.
   (a) What was the result of their experiment? *(3 marks)*
   (b) Explain why the results led to their theory that each atom has a small positive
      nucleus. *(2 marks)*
   (c) Why did this theory become accepted instead of the 'plum pudding' model of
      the atom? *(1 mark)*

31 marks

Examination Questions

1 The diagram represents an atom of lithium.

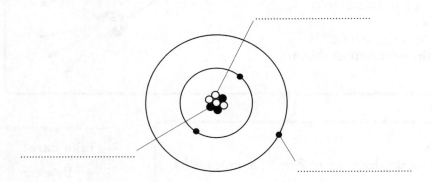

   (a) Complete the diagram by writing in the spaces the name of each type of particle.
      Use only words given in the box. Each word may be used once or not at all.

electron	neutron	nucleus	proton

   (3 marks)

   (b) Which type of particle found inside the atom is uncharged?

   .... *(1 mark)*

(c) What is the mass number of this atom, 3, 4, 7 or 10? ....

Give a reason for your choice.

....

....

(2 marks) 6 marks

2 (a) The diagrams represent three atoms **X**, **Y** and **Z**.

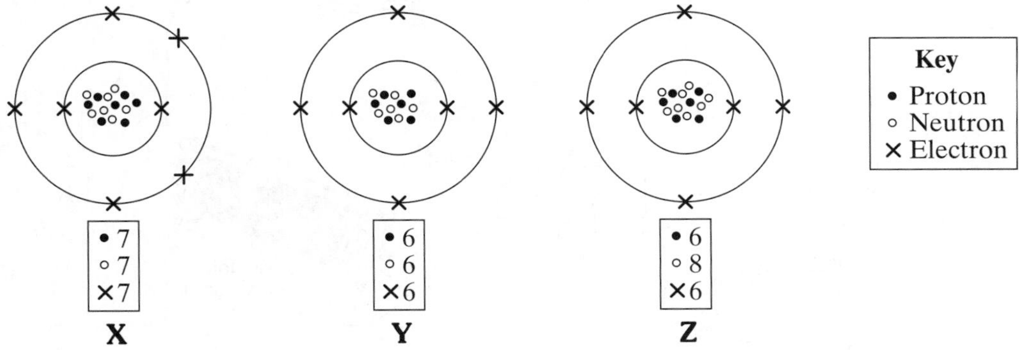

• 7
○ 7
× 7
X
• 6
○ 6
× 6
Y
• 6
○ 8
× 6
Z
Key
• Proton
○ Neutron
× Electron

Which **two** of the atoms are from the same element?

....

Give a reason for your answer.

....

....

(2 marks)

(b) In the early part of the 20th century some scientists investigated the paths taken by positively-charged alpha particles into and out of a very thin piece of gold foil.

A
B
C
Gold nucleus

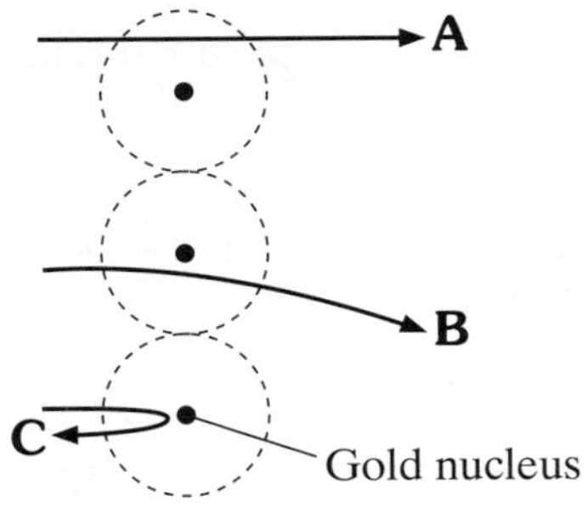

The diagram shows the paths of three alpha particles.
Explain the different paths **A**, **B** and **C** of the alpha particles.

To gain full marks in this question you should write your ideas in good English.

Put them into a sensible order and use the correct scientific words.

....

....

....

....

....

(3 marks) 5 marks

Answers on page 118

Getting the Grades – Electricity

Try this question, then compare your answer with the two examples opposite ▶

The drawing shows the circuit used to investigate how the current through a 5 ohm (Ω) resistor changes as the potential difference (voltage) across the resistor changes.

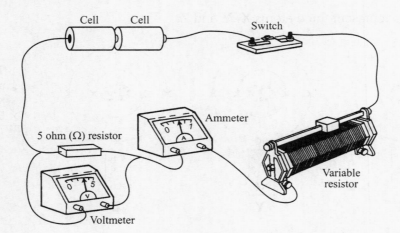

(a) Draw a circuit diagram of this circuit. Use the correct symbols for each part of the circuit.

(2 marks)

(b) (i) Write down the equation that links current, potential difference and resistance.

.... *(1 mark)*

(ii) Calculate the potential difference across the 5 ohm (Ω) resistor when the current through the resistor equals 0.4 A. Show clearly how you work out your final answer.

....

....

potential difference = ...volts

(2 marks)

(iii) Complete the graph to show how the current through the resistor changes as the potential difference across the resistor increases from 0 V to 3 V. Assume the resistor stays at a constant temperature.

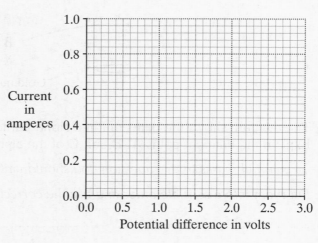

(2 marks)

(c) The resistor is replaced by a 3 V filament lamp. The resistance of the lamp increases as the potential difference across it increases. Why?

....

.... *(1 mark)*

8 marks

GRADE 'A' ANSWER

Ayesha has drawn all of the circuit symbols correctly and has put everything in the correct place in the circuit except the ammeter and the voltmeter, which she has mixed up. She gains one mark.

Ayesha

(a) [circuit diagram] ✓ ✗

Ayesha has also done everything correctly here, so she gains all three marks.

(b) (i) potential difference = current × resistance ✓
   (ii) potential difference = 0.4 V × 5 Ω ✓
        potential difference = 2.0 volts ✓

Ayesha knows that the current–potential difference graph should be a straight line passing through the origin, so gets the first mark. However she does not realise that the line should pass through the point (2.0, 0.4) which she has calculated in part (ii), so she does not get the second mark.

(iii) [graph: Current in amperes vs Potential difference in volts, straight line] ✗ ✓

(c) Because the temperature increases. ✓

Ayesha scores the mark because she has explained why there is a change in the resistance.

6 marks = Grade A answer

▶ **Improve your Grades   A up to A***

Draw circuit diagrams neatly and carefully. Remember that ammeters always go in series and voltmeters always go in parallel. If you sketch a graph think about the values of any coordinates that you may be able to show on the graph.

GRADE 'C' ANSWER

James has drawn the symbol for the variable resistor incorrectly, so he loses the first mark. He has put the voltmeter in parallel with both the 5 ohm resistor **and** the ammeter but this is not what the drawing shows, so he loses the second mark.

James

(a) [circuit diagram] ✗ ✗

James has written the equation and used it correctly to get the right answer, so he gets all of the marks here. He has sensibly shown his working so that he would have gained some credit even if his final answer was wrong.

(b) (i) potential difference = current × resistance ✓
   (ii) potential difference = 0.4 V × 5 Ω ✓
        potential difference = 2.0 volts ✓

The graph should be a straight line but James draws a curve and so does not get either mark.

(iii) [graph: Current in amperes vs Potential difference in volts, curve] ✗ ✗

(c) Because it gets hotter. ✓   James is correct.

4 marks = Grade C answer

▶ **Improve your Grades   C up to B**

Take care with circuit diagrams. Make sure that you know all of the symbols. Learn the graphs of current against potential difference (voltage) for a resistor at a constant temperature, a filament lamp and a diode.

Turning effect of moments

▶ **ThinkAbout:**

1. The turning effect (or . . . .) on a spanner depends upon the . . . . applied and on the . . . . from the nut to the force.

2. The centre of mass (centre of . . . .) of a metre rule is at the . . . . of the rule.
3. An object balances at its centre of . . . .

▶ **Finding the centre of mass of a card**

A suspended object comes to rest with its centre of mass below the pivot. Then the weight does not exert a turning effect (moment).

Hanging the card twice, with a plumbline, allows you to find the centre of mass:

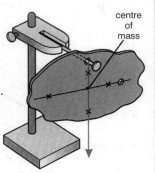

centre of mass

▶ **Stable and unstable objects**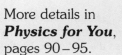

If the line of action of the weight (W) lies outside the base of the object, there is a moment, and the object tends to fall over.

▶ **Calculating moments**

The size of a moment (turning effect) can be calculated by:

moment	=	force	×	perpendicular distance (from line of action to pivot)
(Nm)		(newton, N)		(metre, m)

▶ **The law of moments**

If an object is not turning, the moments must be balanced, so:

In equilibrium:

total anti-clockwise moment	=	total clockwise moment

More details in **Physics for You**, pages 90–95.

Example 1

A metre rule is balanced at its centre. How big is the force X?

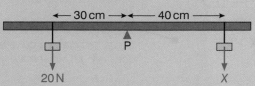

total moment anti-clockwise	=	total moment clockwise

$20\,N \times 30\,cm = X \times 40\,cm$

$\therefore X = \underline{15\,N}$

Example 2 **H**

A metre rule is balanced, but not at its centre. What is the weight (W) of the rule?

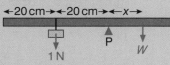

Since W is at the centre, $x = 10$ cm.

total moment anti-clockwise	=	total moment clockwise

$1\,N \times 20\,cm = W \times 10\,cm$

$\therefore W = \underline{2\,N}$

Take care: Make sure you can explain all the steps of the 'card' experiment.

Moving in a circle

> **ThinkAbout:**
>
> 1. The Earth moves in a (nearly) .... orbit round the .... It is held by ....
> 2. Velocity is the same as .... except that it also has a .... It is a .... quantity.
>
> 3. If the velocity of an object is changing, then it is ....
> 4. For a car to turn a corner there must be a .... force between the tyres and the ....

▶ **Circular motion**

In the diagram, if the string breaks, the object moves in a straight line.

To move in a circle there must be a resultant force on it (the tension in the string).

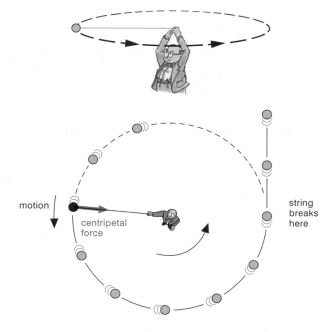

An object moving in a circle at constant **speed** is changing its direction all the time.

This means that its **velocity is changing** all the time (because velocity is a vector quantity, with size and direction).

Because its velocity is changing, it is continuously **accelerating**, towards the centre of the circle!

In order to accelerate it must have a resultant force on it. This is the **centripetal force**, acting towards the centre of the circle.

The centripetal force can be provided by a string, or by friction, or by gravitational attraction, or other forces:

Example:	*Centripetal force is provided by:*
Object whirling in a circle	tension in the string
A car turning a corner	friction between tyres and road
You on car seat as it turns corner	friction between you and the seat
The Earth orbiting the Sun	gravitational attraction of the Sun on the Earth
An electron orbiting an atom	attraction between charges (negative electron and positive nucleus)

▶ **Centripetal force**

The centripetal force will need to be greater if:
- the mass of the object is greater,
- the speed of the object is greater,
- the radius of the circle is smaller.

More details in **Physics for You**, pages 70–71.

Answers:
1. circular, Sun, gravity
2. speed, direction, vector
3. accelerating
4. friction (centripetal, resultant), road

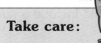

Take care:
Make sure you can name the centripetal force in different examples.

Turning effect of moments; Moving in a circle

Homework Questions

1 Explain what is meant by the term 'moment'. *(1 mark)*

2 Alan pulls a door open with a force of 8 N. The door handle is 0.7 m from the hinge. What is the moment turning the door as it opens? *(2 marks)*

3 Jack and Jill are playing on a see-saw. Jill is heavier than Jack.
   (a) How should Jill change her position to make the see-saw balance? *(2 marks)*
   [H] (b) What is the total effect of the forces when the see-saw is balanced? *(2 marks)*

4 Laura is experimenting with an odd shaped piece of card. She hangs the card from a nail and marks a vertical line. She makes another hole in the card and repeats the experiment.
   (a) What is the name for the place where the lines cross? *(1 mark)*
   (b) How could Laura improve the accuracy of her experiment? *(1 mark)*

5 Scientists at NASA devised a safe way to test the stability of some tall cars. They tied each car on to a centrifuge that could spin it round in large circles. The centrifuge speeded up and when it was going fast enough, the car began to roll over sideways.
   (a) What happens to the centripetal force on the car as the centrifuge turns faster? *(2 marks)*
   [H] (b) Explain why a tall and narrow car is more likely to roll over in this test than a low and wide car. *(2 marks)*
   (c) Explain why a car is more likely to roll over when it is driven at the same speed round a sharper corner. *(2 marks)*
   (d) Explain why it is important to test the stability of a car. *(2 marks)*

17 marks

Examination Questions

1 The diagram shows an ice skater moving in a circle.

Explain how the forces acting on the dancer cause her to follow a circular path. Your answer should include a reference to centripetal force.

....

....

....

(3 marks)

3 marks

2 (a) A thin sheet of cardboard is cut to the shape shown below. Two holes are made in it. A pin is stuck into a cork held in a clamp. The apparatus is used to find the centre of mass of the card.

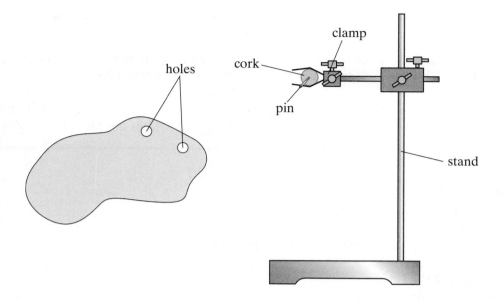

(i) What other piece of equipment is needed?

....

(1 mark)

(ii) *To gain full marks in this question you should write your ideas in good English. Put them into a suitable order and use the correct scientific words.*

Describe how you would use the equipment to find the centre of mass of the card.

....

....

....

....

....

(4 marks)

(b) Label with an **X** the centre of mass of each of the three objects below.

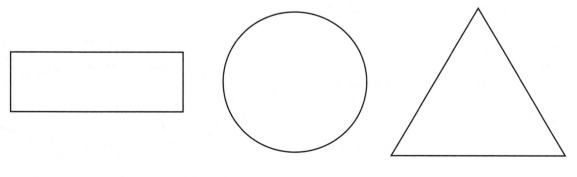

$$\frac{8}{\text{marks}}$$

(3 marks)

Answers on page 118

Planets and satellites

▶ **ThinkAbout:**

1. The Moon orbits the Earth once every . . . .
   It is held in its . . . . by the . . . . pull of the
   . . . .

2. The Earth orbits the Sun once each . . . .
   (. . . . days), held by the . . . . pull.

3. The planets move in . . . . around the . . . .
   We see the planets because they . . . . light
   from the . . . .

4. . . . . can be put in orbit round the Earth.
   They are held in orbit by its . . . . pull.

▶ **Gravitational force**

The Earth, the Sun, the Moon and **all** other bodies
attract each other, with a force called gravity.
The pull of gravity on you, by the Earth, is called your weight.

The bigger the masses of the bodies,
the bigger the force of gravity between them.

As the distance between 2 bodies increases,
the force of gravity decreases.
At twice the distance it is only $\frac{1}{4}$ as much:

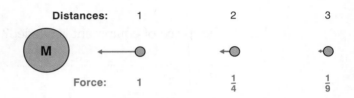

The gravitational force provides the **centripetal force**
needed to keep planets, moons and satellites in their
(nearly) circular orbits, see Topic 19.

▶ **Orbits of planets and comets**

The **planets** are held in orbit round the Sun,
by the gravitational pull of the Sun.
Their orbits are slightly squashed circles (ellipses)
with the Sun quite close to the centre.

To stay in orbit at a particular distance, a planet
must move at a particular speed round the Sun.
The further away a planet is, the longer it takes
to make a complete orbit (eg. Pluto takes 248 years).

Comets are also held in orbit by the
gravitational pull of the Sun.
They have very elliptical orbits, so sometimes
they are near the Sun and sometimes far out in
the Solar System (often beyond Pluto):

Saturn

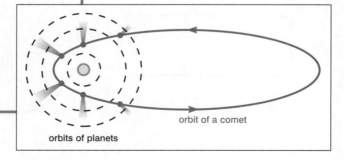

▷ Satellites and gravity

Satellites can be launched to orbit the Earth.
They stay in orbit because of the combination of
the high speed and the force of gravity of the Earth.

To stay in a particular orbit, they have to travel at
the right speed:

The higher the satellite, the **slower** the speed and
the **longer** it takes for one orbit.

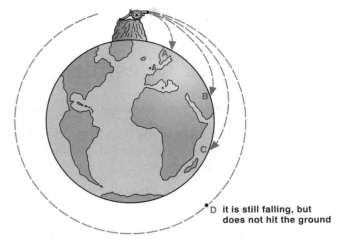

D it is still falling, but
does not hit the ground

*Satellites must travel fast enough
for the orbit they are in*

▷ Uses of satellites

- Monitoring or observation satellites
  eg. weather satellites, military (spy) satellites.

- Communications satellites
  eg. for transmitting telephone calls and
  TV programmes. See also Topic 6.

- Astronomical satellites
  eg. space telescopes taking photos outside
  the Earth's atmosphere. See also Topic 8.

▷ Satellite orbits

Satellites can be launched into **polar** orbit or
equatorial orbit.

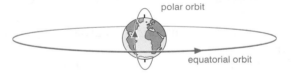

polar orbit

equatorial orbit

Monitoring satellites are usually put into a **low
polar** orbit, so that as the Earth spins beneath
them they can scan different parts of the Earth.

Communication satellites are usually put into
a **high** orbit above the equator.

The height is adjusted so that the satellite
moves round at *exactly the same rate as the
Earth spins. ie. once every 24 hours.*
This means that the satellite is always in the
same position when viewed from Earth.
This is a **geostationary** orbit.

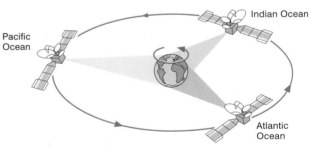

Indian Ocean

Pacific
Ocean

Atlantic
Ocean

*The whole Earth can be covered by
just three geostationary satellites*

Take care:

- When explaining about orbits, make sure
  you use the idea of gravitational force.

- Be clear about the two main kinds of satellites.

- You may be given a table of data about planets
  and asked to interpret the data.

More details in **Physics for You**,
pages 148–149, 153–155, 211, 314.

Planets and satellites

Homework Questions

1 A satellite is in a geostationary orbit. How long will it take to orbit the Earth once? *(1 mark)*

2 Mars orbits closer to the Sun than does Saturn. Jupiter orbits between Mars and Saturn. Which of the planets Mars, Jupiter or Saturn takes the longest time to complete one orbit? *(1 mark)*

3 Explain why satellites that are designed to monitor the whole Earth are usually put into a low polar orbit. *(2 marks)*

4 An astronaut is weightless in a space shuttle. She lets a grape, an apple and an orange float in the air.
(a) In which direction will the force of gravity act between the objects? *(1 mark)*
(b) Which two objects will have the largest gravitational force acting between them? *(2 marks)*

5 The space shuttle is orbiting 320 km above the surface of the Earth.
(a) What happens to the time it takes for it to go around the Earth once if the space shuttle climbs to a higher orbit? *(2 marks)*
(b) What happens to the radius of the orbit if the space shuttle speeds up a little? *(2 marks)*

6 Mercury is the planet nearest to the Sun. It takes 88 days to complete its orbit. The average radius of the orbit of Mercury is 58 million km.
(The circumference of a circle is $2 \times \pi \times r$.)
(a) What provides the centripetal force that keeps Mercury in orbit around the Sun? *(2 marks)*
(b) Why is the radius of Mercury's orbit not given exactly but as an average value? *(2 marks)*
(c) Calculate the orbital speed of Mercury, assuming its orbit is a circle. *(3 marks)*

$$\overline{18}$$ marks

Examination Question

The diagram shows a satellite in orbit around the Earth.

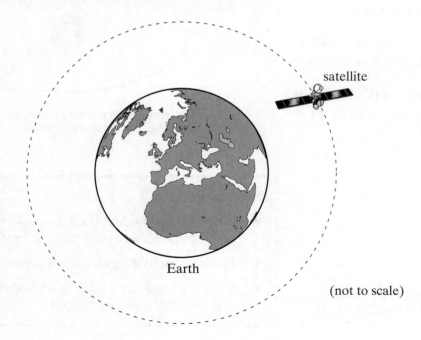

satellite

Earth

(not to scale)

(a) (i) Explain why the satellite stays in orbit.

....

....

....

(2 marks)

(ii) The satellite is boosted to a higher orbit. What effect will this have on the time the satellite takes to complete one orbit?

....

....

....

(1 mark)

(b) Communication satellites send information between places which are a long way apart on Earth.

(i) In what type of orbit are communications satellites usually placed?

....

(1 mark)

(ii) Explain why they are placed in this type of orbit.

....

....

....

(1 mark)

(c) Monitoring satellites are used to monitor conditions on Earth, including the weather.

(i) In what type of orbit are weather satellites usually placed?

....

(1 mark)

(ii) Explain why they are placed in this type of orbit.

....

....

....

(1 mark)

7 marks

Answers on page 118

 **and LENSES**

▷ **ThinkAbout:**

1. At any mirror, the angle of incidence is . . . . to the angle of . . . .

2. When light travels into a glass block, the rays are bent (or . . . .) . . . . the normal line.

▷ **Reflection**

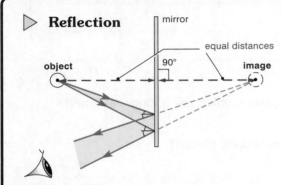

The **image** formed in a plane mirror is:
- the same size as the object,
- upright (erect),
- laterally inverted (left to right),
- virtual (you can't show it on a screen).

▷ **Refraction**

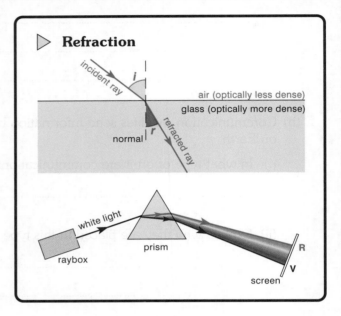

▷ **Curved mirrors**

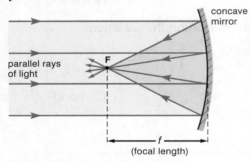

A **concave** mirror *converges* rays.

The image formed by a concave mirror depends on where the object is. The diagram below shows 2 constructions.

① Rays parallel to the axis are reflected through F, the principal focus,

② A ray travelling to the centre of the mirror is reflected so that: angle of incidence = angle of reflection.

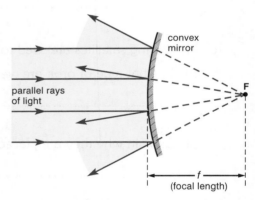

A **convex** mirror *diverges* rays.

The image in a convex mirror is *always*:
- virtual
- diminished (smaller)
- upright (erect).

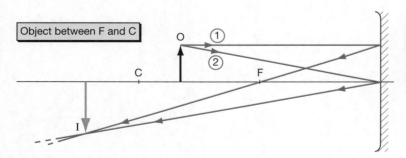

Object between F and C

Image
– outside C
– inverted
  magnified
  real

▷ Lenses

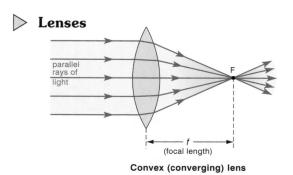

Convex (converging) lens

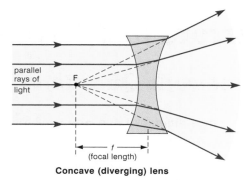

Concave (diverging) lens

The image formed by a **converging** lens depends on where the object is (see the diagrams below).

The image formed by a **diverging** lens is *always*:
- virtual
- diminished (smaller)
- upright (erect).

Images in mirrors and lenses can be:
- real or virtual,
- inverted or upright (erect)
- magnified (enlarged) or diminished.

$$\text{magnification} = \frac{\text{height of image I}}{\text{height of object O}}$$

The diagrams below are drawn using 2 constructions:

① Rays parallel to the axis are refracted to go through the principal focus F.
② Rays of light going through the centre of the lens travel straight on.

▷ In a camera

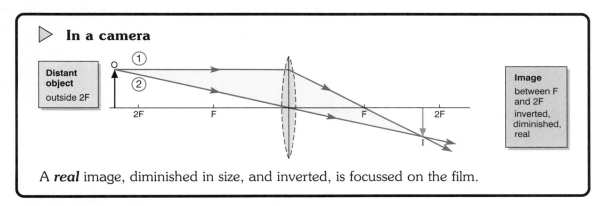

A *real* image, diminished in size, and inverted, is focussed on the film.

▷ In a magnifying glass

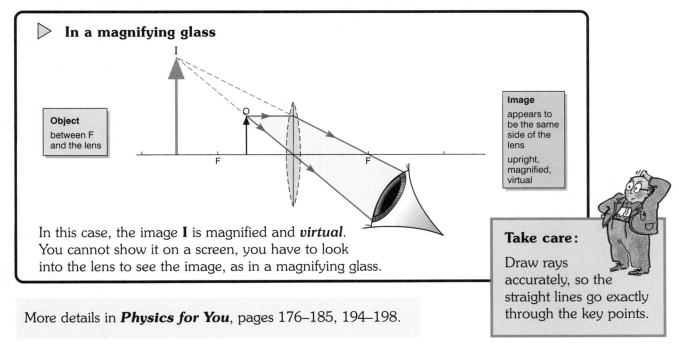

In this case, the image **I** is magnified and *virtual*. You cannot show it on a screen, you have to look into the lens to see the image, as in a magnifying glass.

Take care:

Draw rays accurately, so the straight lines go exactly through the key points.

More details in **Physics for You**, pages 176–185, 194–198.

Mirrors and Lenses

Homework Questions

1 Give **one** difference and **one** similarity between the images formed by a plane mirror and a convex mirror. *(2 marks)*

2 Draw a diagram to show how parallel rays of light from the Sun are focused by a concave mirror. Mark the focal length on your diagram. *(3 marks)*

3 Lenses and prisms can bend the light rays that pass through them. Name the term used to describe this sort of bending. *(1 mark)*

4 Draw a diagram of a plane mirror reflecting a light ray. Label the incident ray, the reflected ray and the normal. Make it clear which two angles are equal. *(4 marks)*

5 Rashid takes a picture of his house using a digital camera.
The house is 8 m high, but its image in the camera is 0.008 m high and upside down.
(a) What type of lens is used in a camera? *(1 mark)*
(b) Give a full description of the image in the camera. *(1 mark)*
(c) Explain how an image is formed in the camera.
(You may draw a diagram to explain this if you prefer.) *(3 marks)*
(d) Calculate the magnification of the image. *(3 marks)*
(e) Explain why there is no unit for magnification. *(1 mark)*
(f) Rashid moves much nearer to the house to take another picture of it. The camera refocuses automatically. How does this affect the magnification of the image? *(3 marks)*

6 There are two types of optical telescope: refracting telescopes and reflecting telescopes. Suggest which optical components each type might contain. *(2 marks)*

24 marks

Examination Question

(a) The diagram shows how parallel rays of light pass through a convex lens.

(i) Mark the position of the focus.

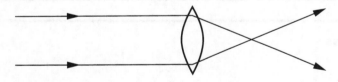

(1 mark)

(ii) Is this a **converging** lens, a **diverging** lens, **both** or **neither**?

....

(1 mark)

(b) The diagram shows how parallel rays of light pass through a concave lens.

(i) Mark the position of the focus.

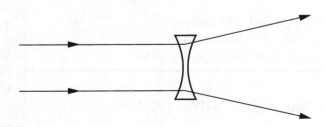

(1 mark)

(ii) Is this a **converging** lens, a **diverging** lens, **both** or **neither**?

....

(1 mark)

(c) Complete these sentences by crossing out the two lines in each box that are wrong.

In a camera, a
| converging |
| diverging |
| parallel |
lens is used to produce an image of an

object on a
| film |
| lens |
| screen |
. The image is
| larger than |
| smaller than |
| the same size as |
the object.

The image is
| further from |
| nearer to |
| the same distance from |
the lens, compared to the distance of the

object from the lens.

(4 marks)

(d) In a cinema projector, a convex lens is used to produce a *magnified*, *real* image.

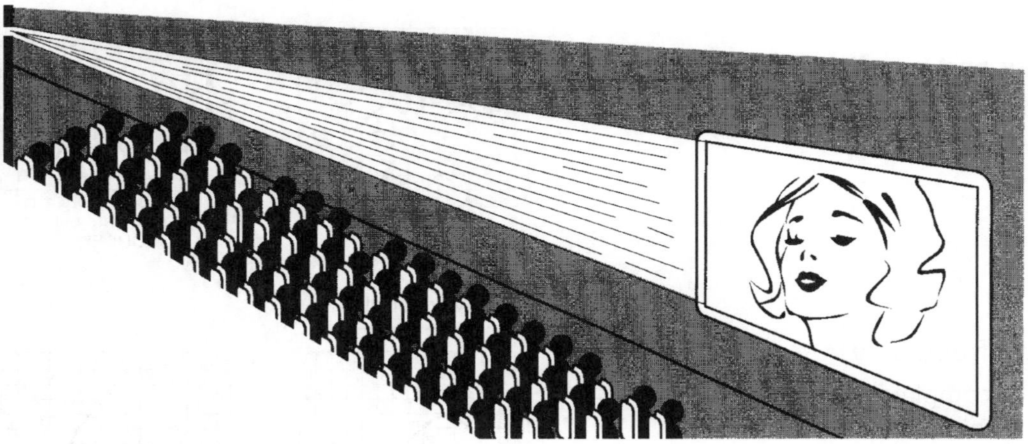

(i) What does *magnified* mean?

....

....

(1 mark)

(ii) What is a *real* image?

....

....

(1 mark)

10 marks

Answers on page 119

> ### ThinkAbout:

1. All . . . . are caused by vibrations.
2. The speed of sound in air is about 340 . . . . per second.
3. Like other waves, a sound wave transfers . . . . without transferring any matter.

4. Echoes are due to the . . . . of sound.
5. Sound can travel through solids, ... , and . . . . It cannot travel through a . . . .
6. A sound wave is a . . . . wave. The . . . . is transferred from molecule to . . . .

> ### Using an oscilloscope
The waveform of a sound can be displayed using a microphone and an oscilloscope:

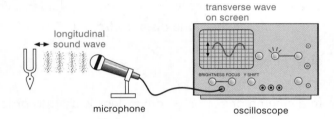

microphone   oscilloscope

> ### Loudness and amplitude
The greater the amplitude of the vibrations, the louder the sound:

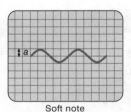

Soft note

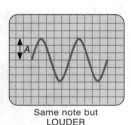

Same note but LOUDER

> ### Pitch and frequency
The number of complete vibrations in each second is called the frequency. It is measured in hertz (Hz).

The higher the frequency, the higher the pitch of the sound:

wavelength

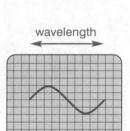

Low pitch
(low frequency)
long wavelength

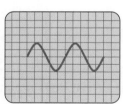

High pitch
(high frequency)
short wavelength

> ### Quality of the sound
Different musical instruments sound different even if they play the same note. They have a different tone or **quality**.
This depends on the waveform of the sound:

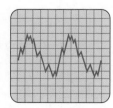

A note on a violin

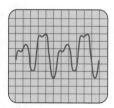

The same note on a piano

Answers:

1. sounds   2. metres   3. energy   4. reflection   5. liquids, gases, vacuum
6. longitudinal, energy, molecule

▷ Ultrasonic waves (ultrasound)

The normal range of hearing for humans can be 20 Hz to 20 000 Hz.

Sound waves with a higher frequency than this are called ultrasonic waves.
Because they have a high frequency, they have a short wavelength.

▷ Uses of ultrasound

Ultrasonic waves can be used:
- in industry for quality control eg. to detect flaws in metal castings,
- in medicine eg. pre-natal scanning (ultrasound is safer than X-rays),
- in industry for cleaning dirty objects eg. watches, street lamp covers.

▷ Reflections

When ultrasonic waves meet a boundary between
two different media, the waves are partly reflected back.
The time taken for the reflections (echoes) to reach a detector
can be used to measure how far away the boundary is.
The results can be shown on a visual display.

▷ Detecting flaws in a metal casting

A transmitter is sending out pulses
of ultrasonic waves:
A receiver picks up the echoes from
different parts of the metal and
shows the results on an oscilloscope.

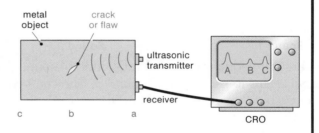

Pulse A is the transmitted pulse.
Pulse B has been reflected by
the flaw (b) in the metal.
Pulse C is the reflected pulse from
the end (c) of the metal block.

▷ Pre-natal scanning

When an ultrasonic wave
travels from one substance
to another (skin, muscle,
bone, fluid) most of the
wave is refracted through,
but some is reflected back.

The information is used
to build up a picture of
the fetus:

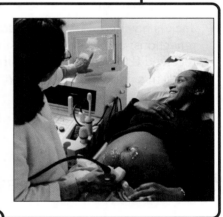

▷ Ultrasonic cleaning

Ultrasonic waves can be
used to shake loose the dirt
on delicate mechanisms,
without having to take them
to pieces.

Cleaning a watch

liquid in tank

Take care:

Be careful not
to confuse
sound waves
(longitudinal) with
electromagnetic waves
(transverse), see also
Topic 6.

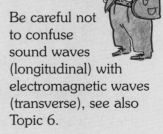

More details in *Physics for You*, pages 224–230, 232–233.

Sound; Ultrasound

Homework Questions

1 Name the unit for frequency. *(1 mark)*

2 What is the relationship between the pitch and the frequency of a sound? *(1 mark)*

3 Explain what is meant by the term 'quality of a sound.' *(2 marks)*

4 Give **three** similarities and **one** difference between sound waves and ultrasound waves. *(4 marks)*

5 Annabel used an oscilloscope to investigate some sounds. She kept the same oscilloscope settings each time. She took these photographs of the traces for three different sounds:

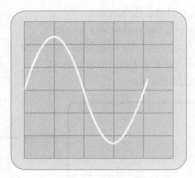  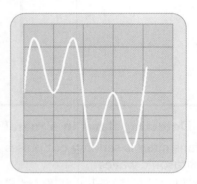

Sound 1   **Sound 2**   **Sound 3**

(a) Compare the frequency and the amplitude of sound 1 and sound 2. *(2 marks)*

(b) Annabel listens to sound 1 and sound 3. She can hear that the sounds have the same frequency, but there is some other difference. Explain this difference. *(2 marks)*

(c) The oscilloscope time base is set to '25 μs per division'. This means that one square represents 0.000 025 second.
Calculate the frequency of sound 2 and explain why Annabel cannot hear it. *(4 marks)*

H **6** Jack is having an ultrasound scan to locate a kidney stone. The probe receives two reflections: one from Jack's skin and another from the stone. The second reflection is received 0.0001 second after the first. The speed of ultrasound waves in human tissue is 1500 m/s. How far was the kidney stone beneath Jack's skin? *(4 marks)*

20 marks

Examination Questions

1 (a) Complete the following sentence:

Sound is produced when an object ....

(1 mark)

(b) Choose words from the list to complete the following sentences:

higher   louder   lower   quieter

(i) If the frequency is increased, the pitch of the sound becomes ....

(ii) If its amplitude is increased, the sound becomes ....

(2 marks)

(c) The diagram shows a pre-natal scan.

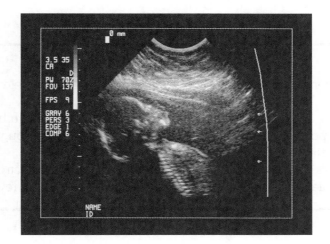

(i) What type of waves are used for pre-natal scanning?

....

(1 mark)

(ii) Explain why we cannot hear these waves.

....

....

....

(2 marks)

6 marks

2 The diagram shows how ultrasonic waves can be used to clean a watch.

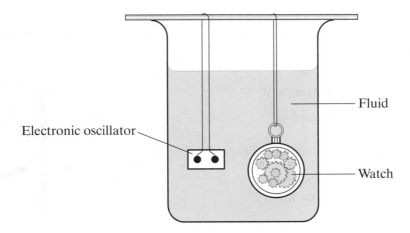

Suggest how this method cleans the watch.

....

....

....

....

(2 marks)

2 marks

Answers on page 119

Movement from electricity

> **Magnetic fields**

There is a magnetic field between the poles of a magnet:

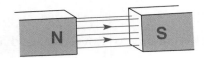

A wire carrying a current also produces a magnetic field:

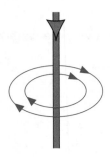

If the wire (carrying a current) is put between the poles of the magnet, the 2 magnetic fields interact, and exert a force (see below). This is called the **motor effect**.

The wire tries to move from the stronger part of the field (shown by the lines of force) to the weaker part.

> **The motor effect**

If a wire carrying a current cuts *across* a magnetic field, it experiences a **force** on it.

The size of the force can be increased by:
- increasing the current,
- increasing the strength of the magnetic field.

The direction of the force will be reversed if the direction of *either* the current *or* the field is reversed.

This effect is used in electric motors, loud-speakers, etc. (see the opposite page.)

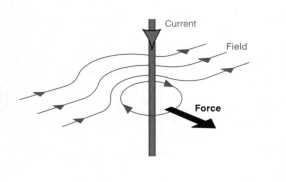

Note that the wire has to cut across the field of the magnet. If the wire is parallel to the field, then there is *no* force.

▷ The electric motor

In the diagram, the electric motor has:
- a permanent magnet,
- a coil through which a current is flowing.

Because of the motor effect (see the opposite page), each side of the coil has a force on it.
The force is **up** on one side and **down** on the other side.
This makes the coil rotate.

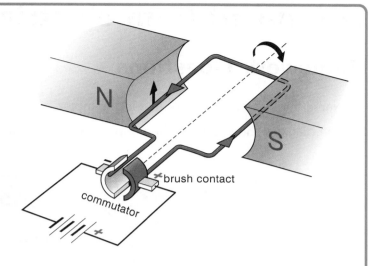

The motor can be made more powerful by:
- increasing the current,
- increasing the number of turns on the coil,
- using a stronger magnet.

A motor transforms electrical energy to kinetic energy. See also Topic 4.

Electric motors are used in hair-dryers, washing-machines, vacuum cleaners, fridges, fans, clocks, DVD-players, windscreen wipers, lifts, escalators, etc.

▷ The loudspeaker

A loudspeaker changes electrical signals into sound waves.
The signals pass through a wire which is in a magnetic field:

When the current flows one way. the motor effect pushes the coil (and the cone) **in**.
When the current reverses, the cone moves **out**.

If the electrical signal varies at 1000 hertz, you will hear a sound of frequency 1000 Hz.

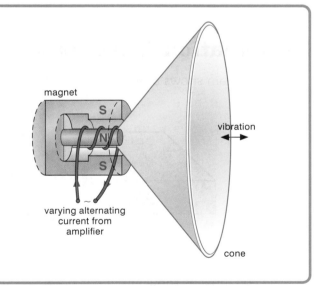

More details in **Physics for You**, pages 286, 290–293.

Take care:

You may be given a diagram of an electrical device, and asked to explain how the motor effect is used in it.

Movement from electricity

Homework Questions

1 Name three devices that use an electric motor. *(3 marks)*

2 The diagram shows some of the parts of an electric motor.

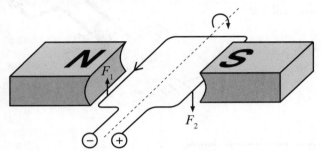

(a) What is the direction of the magnetic field in the diagram? *(1 mark)*
(b) What is the *effect* of reversing the magnetic field? *(2 marks)*
(c) What is the effect of reversing the magnetic field **and** reversing the current? *(1 mark)*
(d) Explain why the two forces F_1 and F_2 act in opposite directions. *(2 marks)*
(e) Suggest two changes that would increase the forces F_1 and F_2. *(2 marks)*

3 Amy is experimenting with a loudspeaker and a battery.
When she connects the battery, the cone moves to the left.
What happens if:
(a) she reverses the battery connections,
(b) she uses an a.c. power supply instead of the battery,
(c) she replaces the magnet with a stronger one, and
(d) she winds more turns of wire on the coil?

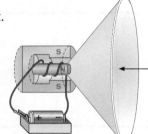

$$\frac{}{15}$$ marks

(4 marks)

Examination Questions

1 The diagram shows a simple electric motor.

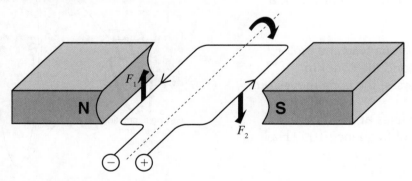

The coil turns as shown in the diagram.
(a) State **two** ways of reversing the direction of forces F_1 and F_2.

   1. ....

     ....

   2. ....

     ....

(2 marks)

(b) Give **two** ways in which the size of the forces can be increased.

1. ....

....

2. ....

....

(2 marks)

$\dfrac{4}{\text{marks}}$

2 Sam is investigating the force on a wire in a magnetic field. She puts a straight wire between two magnets and passes a current through the wire.

wire

N   S

θ

She changes the angle (θ) between the current and the field and then measures the force on the wire. These are her results:

Angle in degrees	0	20	40	60	80	100	120	140	160
Force in N	0.00	0.21	0.39	0.52	0.59	0.59	0.52	0.39	0.21

(a) Which is the dependent variable? ....

(1 mark)

(b) Plot a graph of force against angle.

(4 marks)

Force in N

0.70
0.60
0.50
0.40
0.30
0.20
0.10
0.00

0   20   40   60   80   100   120   140   160   180

Angle in degrees

(c) There is most force when the angle is ....

(1 mark)

(d) Explain what force will act when the angle is increased to 180°.

....

....

(2 marks)

$\dfrac{8}{\text{marks}}$

Answers on page 119

ELECTRO-MAGNETIC INDUCTION

▷ Producing electricity

If a magnet is moved into this coil of wire, a current is produced ('induced') in the coil circuit.
It is converting kinetic energy to electrical energy.

If the other pole of the magnet is moved into the coil, the direction of the current is reversed.
If the magnet is moved out of the coil, the current is reversed.

The same effect occurs if the coil is moved instead of the magnet.

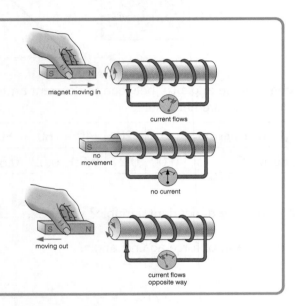

magnet moving in

current flows

no movement

no current

moving out

current flows opposite way

▷ An a.c. generator (or 'alternator' or 'dynamo')

A generator consists of a coil rotating in a magnetic field (or a magnet rotating in a coil):

When the wires of the coil 'cut through' the magnetic field lines, a voltage (p.d.) is produced between the ends of the wire.

This induced voltage can be increased by:
● using a coil with more turns,
● using a stronger magnet,
● rotating the coil faster,
● using a coil with a larger area.

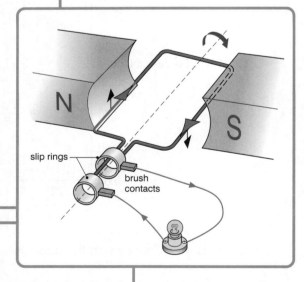

slip rings

brush contacts

 In the diagram, the rotating coil cuts the magnetic field, inducing a current in the circuit. The slip-rings and brushes are used to connect the coil to the lamp while the coil is turning.

▷ Transformers

Transformers are used to change the voltage of
an a.c. supply. They do not work with d.c.
They are used in the National Grid (see below).

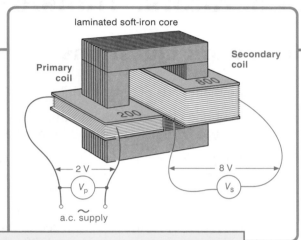

laminated soft-iron core

Secondary coil

Primary coil

A transformer consists of 2 separate coils,
wound on an iron core:

When an alternating voltage (p.d.) is applied
across the primary coil, it produces a
changing magnetic field.
This changing magnetic field induces an
alternating voltage across the secondary coil.

The voltages are connected by:

$$\frac{\text{voltage across primary}}{\text{voltage across secondary}} = \frac{\text{number of turns on primary}}{\text{number of turns on secondary}} \quad \boxed{H}$$

Example $\boxed{H}$

A transformer has a primary coil with 200 turns, and
a secondary coil with 800 turns (a 'step-up' transformer).
If the primary voltage is 2 V (a.c.), what is the secondary voltage?

Substituting the numbers in the equation shown above,

$$\frac{2\text{ V}}{\text{voltage across secondary}} = \frac{200}{800}$$

So: $\quad \dfrac{\text{voltage across secondary}}{2\text{ V}} = \dfrac{800}{200}$ (by inverting both sides)

$\therefore \quad$ voltage across secondary $= \dfrac{800}{200} \times 2\text{ V} = \underline{8\text{ V}}$ (a.c.)

▷ The National Grid

At power stations, step-up transformers are used to produce very high voltages,
before the electricity is distributed by power lines (the National Grid).
Local step-down transformers reduce the voltage to safer levels for homes.

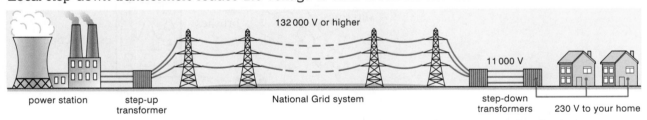

132 000 V or higher

11 000 V

power station   step-up
transformer

National Grid system

step-down
transformers   230 V to your home

The higher the voltage, the smaller the current needed
to transfer energy at the same rate. So less energy is
wasted in heating up the power lines.

Take care:

Remember that a
voltage is only induced
when something moves
or changes (a wire or a
magnetic field).

More details in ***Physics for You***, pages 296–303.

Electromagnetic induction, Generators; Transformers

Homework Questions

1 Name the main parts of a transformer. *(3 marks)*

2 A mobile phone charger plugs into the mains. It is designed to charge a 5 V battery. Name the type of transformer used in the charger. *(1 mark)*

3 This rechargeable torch contains a strong magnet that can slide in and out of a coil of wire. When the torch is shaken up and down, a potential difference is induced. Electrical energy is stored in a capacitor and then used to light a LED.

(a) What type of current will be induced in the coil? *(1 mark)*
(b) Describe the effect on the potential difference of the following actions:
    (i)   Shaking the torch faster.
    (ii) Replacing the magnet with a weaker one.
    (iii) Adding more turns of wire to the coil, wound in the same direction.
    (iv) Adding more turns of wire to the coil, wound in the opposite direction. *(4 marks)*

4 Matt needed three new batteries for his torch, but he could only find one.
He tried to use a step-up transformer in this circuit to increase the battery voltage:
Explain why Matt's plan did not work. *(2 marks)*

[H] 5 Using the diagram on page 104, explain the purpose of the slip rings and brushes in a simple a.c. generator. *(2 marks)*

[H] 6 A mains transformer is designed to provide 12 V for a radio. The primary coil is connected to the 230 V mains and has 4600 turns. How many turns are on the secondary coil? *(2 marks)*

15 marks

Examination Questions

1 The diagram shows a simple generator. The trace on the oscilloscope shows that the generator produces an alternating current.

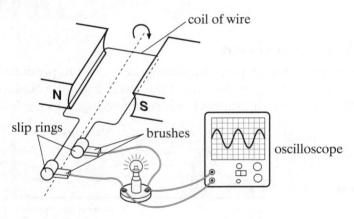

coil of wire

N   S

slip rings

brushes

oscilloscope

What should be done to make the generator give the oscilloscope trace drawn opposite?
Assume the controls on the oscilloscope are unchanged.

....

....

....

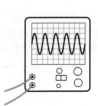

(2 marks)

2 marks

2 The diagram shows how electrical energy is transmitted from a power station to the consumer.

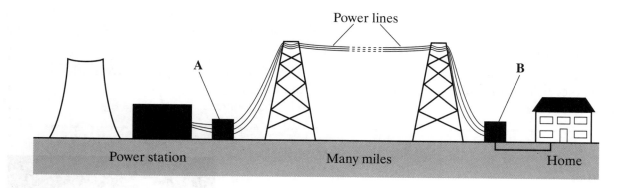

(a) (i) What is the purpose of Transformer **A**?

....

....

....

(2 marks)

(ii) Why is it necessary to have Transformer **B** between the power lines and the consumer?

....

....

....

....

(2 marks)

(b) Explain, as fully as you can, why electricity is transmitted at very high voltages through the power lines.

....

....

....

....

(3 marks)

(c) Explain why these transformers only work using alternating current (a.c.).

....

....

....

....

(2 marks)

9
marks

Answers on page 120

The Life of a Star

▶ **ThinkAbout:**

1. Our nearest star is the . . . .
2. A group of billions of stars, like the Milky Way, is called a . . . .

3. The Universe is thought to have started in the Big . . . .
   This happened . . . . of years ago.

▶ **Galaxies**

Our Sun is one of billions of stars in our Milky Way galaxy.
The Universe as a whole is made of billions of galaxies.

Within a galaxy the stars are often millions of times farther apart than the planets in our Solar System.
And the galaxies are often million of times farther apart than the stars within a galaxy.

▶ **The birth of a star**

Most scientists believe that the planets were formed at the same time as the Sun.

It began with a huge cloud of dust and gas called a *nebula*.
The gas was mostly hydrogen, with some helium. These gases make up most of the Universe.

Because of gravitational attraction between the particles, the cloud began to shrink.
As it got smaller and smaller, it got hotter and hotter.

Eventually the temperature was so high that *nuclear fusion* began (see opposite page).
It became the star we call the Sun.
Other stars form in the same way.

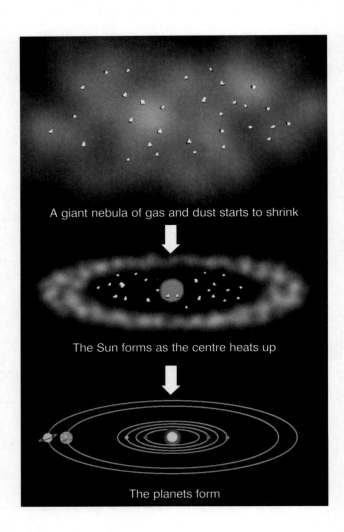

A giant nebula of gas and dust starts to shrink

The Sun forms as the centre heats up

The planets form

Meanwhile the planets began to form from the dust and gases.
They are kept in orbit by the gravitational attraction of the Sun.

Answers: 1. Sun   2. galaxy   3. Bang, billions

▶ Making new elements

The energy of a star is produced by nuclear fusion (like a hydrogen bomb). See Topic 17.

The nuclei of lighter elements (mainly hydrogen and helium) fuse together, to produce nuclei of new (heavier) elements.

In a stable star like the Sun, 2 forces are balanced:
- the force of gravity (inwards) trying to crush the star,
- forces of expansion (outwards) due to radiation pressure.

Stars eventually use up their fuel and start to change. What happens then depends on the mass of the star.

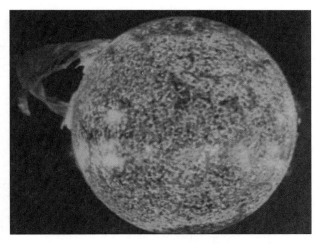

An ultra-violet photo of the Sun

▶ The life and death of a star

As a star gets older, it expands to become a red giant or a red supergiant, as shown:

A red supergiant may contract and then explode as a **supernova**: $\boxed{\text{H}}$

During this explosion, heavy elements such as gold are formed, and thrown out across space ... and later become the dust for making new stars and planets (and human beings).

Later the dying star contracts to form a dwarf star, or a neutron star, or a black hole:
Its matter is extremely dense.

Small mass

yellow dwarf
(like our Sun)
↓
red giant
↓
white dwarf
↓
black dwarf

Large mass

blue giant
↓
red supergiant
↓
supernova
↓   ↓
neutron   black
star   hole

In extreme cases, the star is so dense, and the pull of gravity so strong, that nothing can escape from it, not even light. It is a **black hole**.

We can't see a black hole, but we may see its effect (eg. X-rays are emitted when matter spirals into it, see also 'Observing the Universe' in Topic 8).

Take care:

- Be clear about the two main life-cycles of stars.
- Do not confuse nuclear fusion with nuclear fission (Topic 17).
- Be clear about where all the elements come from.

More details in **Physics for You**, pages 152, 156–157.

The Life of a Star

Homework Questions

1 Name our galaxy. *(1 mark)*

2 Place these in order of size, with the smallest first:
   galaxy, Universe, star. *(1 mark)*

3 In a star, the inward and outward forces are balanced. Explain what causes
   these forces. *(2 marks)*

4 Describe the stages in the formation of a star. (You may draw a diagram if
   you prefer.) *(4 marks)*

5 Explain why stars are able to go on producing energy for millions of years. *(2 marks)*

6 Describe the stages in the life cycle of a yellow dwarf star like our Sun. *(4 marks)*

7 Explain why our Sun is
   (a) likely to become a red giant, but
   (b) unlikely to become a supernova. *(4 marks)*

8 There can be two alternative outcomes of a supernova.
   (a) Name the two different objects that could be produced. *(2 marks)*
   (b) Explain the difference between these objects. *(2 marks)*

[H] 9 The early Universe is thought to have contained only hydrogen. Now there are lots of
   different chemical elements.
   (a) Describe the process that formed the heavier elements from hydrogen. *(2 marks)*
   (b) Explain how these elements have become spread throughout the Universe. *(1 mark)*

   25 marks

Examination Questions

1 The following sentences describe the stages that a star such as the Sun goes through during
   its life.

   A The star is stable.

   B The star contracts to a white dwarf.

   C The star expands into a red giant.

   D The star is formed when the force of gravity pulls dust and gases together.

   (a) Arrange the sentences in the order in which the stages happen.

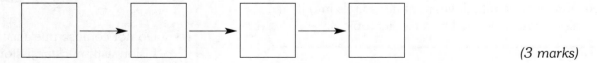

   (3 marks)

   (b) The Sun is at which stage in its life, **A**, **B**, **C** or **D**?

   ....

   (1 mark)

   4 marks

2 *To gain full marks for this question you should write your ideas in good English, put them into a sensible order and use correct scientific words.*

(a) The Sun is at a stable stage of its life.
Explain, in terms of the forces acting on the Sun, what this means.

....

....

....

....

....

(3 marks)

(b) At the end of the stable stage of its life a star will change.
Describe and explain the changes that could take place, for a star:

(i) to become a white dwarf;

....

....

....

....

....

(3 marks)

(ii) to become a black hole.

....

....

....

....

....

(3 marks)

9

marks

3 (a) Explain how stars produce energy.

....

....

....

....

(2 marks)

H (b) What evidence is there to suggest that the Sun was formed from the material produced when an earlier star exploded?

....

....

(1 mark)

3

marks

Answers on page 120

Examination answers and tips

TOPIC 1 – How Science works   (pages 10–11)

Homework questions

1 (a) reproducible   1
   (b) continuous   1
   (c) categoric   1
2 valid data is data which is reliable   1
   and relevant   1
3 to improve the reliability   1
4 *Any two from:* text books, other people's readings, Internet,
   scientific publications   2
5 (a) line-graph   1
   (b) bar chart   1
6 (a) 11.5 m/s to 15.0 m/s   1
   (b) 13.2 m/s   1

Examination questions

1 (a) because she kept it the same to ensure a fair test   1
   (b) (i) because she changes this value step by step (to see
             what happens)   1
        (ii) because you can only have a whole number of layers   1
   (c)

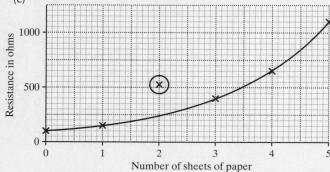

        correct plotting   3
   (d) (i) the point (2, 520)   1
        (ii) curved line of best fit   1
        (iii) 250 Ω (± 50 Ω)   1
2 (a) *Any two points from:*
        he only took one reading; he may not have scientific training;
        he may be influenced by commercial bias (the newspaper
        company); his equipment may be faulty.   2
   (b) *Any two points from:*
        she may be influenced by commercial bias (the power station
        constructors); radiation levels are variable; her equipment
        may be faulty.   2

TOPIC 2 – Conduction, Convection, Radiation

Homework questions   (pages 14–15)

1 heat   1
2 they have free electrons which can move,
   transferring energy to cooler parts   2
3 solids cannot flow   1
4 (a) trapped air and fur are good insulators – so conduction
        is reduced
        air is trapped and cannot move – so convection is reduced
        fur is white – so radiation is reduced   3
   (b) temperature difference is less – so heat is transferred more
        slowly   1
5 *any three from:*
   double-glazing, thick carpet, thick curtains, draught excluder,
   cavity wall insulation, loft insulation   3

6 (a) energy transferred by conduction when particles collide
        energy transferred by convection currents in the water   2
   (b) light coloured surface reduces energy lost by radiation   1
   (c) heating from below helps convection to take place must
        cover the element with water to transfer the heat   2
7 (a) air trapped between the glass layers is an insulator   1
   (b) it provides extra sound insulation
        it improves security   2
   (c) checking the heating bills before and after fitting
        double-glazing, to see if he is using less energy
   or comparing the times needed for the room to warm up
        before and after fitting double-glazing, to see if it warms
        more quickly   1

Examination question

   (a) its temperature   1
   (b) *Effect:* potatoes in blackened foil cool more quickly
        Reason: black surfaces are good radiators (good emitters)   2

Examiner's Tip ✓

*Dark matt surfaces are good absorbers and good emitters of
heat radiation.*
Light shiny surfaces are poor absorbers and poor emitters.

Multiple choice questions

1 1B, 2A, 3D, 4C   4   7   C   1
2 C   1   8   C   1
3 D   1   9   D   1
4 C   1   10 B   1
5 B   1   11 A   1
6 A   1

TOPIC 3 – Energy transfers   (pages 18–19)
Homework questions

1 joule (J)   1
2 it is a number (or a ratio or a percentage)   1
3 heat (thermal energy)   1
4 food (chemical) → work → potential → kinetic
   → electrical → sound
   (thermal energy wasted at each stage)   5
5 (a) Sankey diagram as on page 16, labelled:
        input = 100 J
        light energy = 12 J
        wasted energy = 88 J   3
   (b) LED lamp uses energy more slowly   1
6 (a) 0.47, 0.51, 0.55, 0.58, 0.60   3
   (b) independent variable = weight lifted   1
        control variable = height lifted   1
   (c)

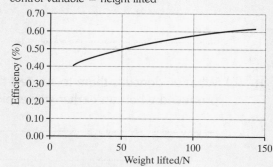

        axes correct and all plotting   4
   (d) efficiency increases with larger weights   1

Examination question

(a) heat   1
(b) it will increase the temperature of the air around it   1
(c) efficiency = 120 J ÷ 200 J
    efficiency = 0.6   2

Examiner's Tip ✓

Efficiencies are often expressed as percentages.
An efficiency of 0.6 is the same as 60%.
Efficiency is a ratio and doesn't have a unit.

Multiple choice questions

1	1C, 2B, 3A, 4D	4		6	B		1
2	A	1		7	D		1
3	A	1		8	C		1
4	D	1		9	C		1
5	(a) B	1					
	(b) C	1					

TOPIC 4 – Using electricity   (pages 22–23)
Homework questions

1 the watt (or kilowatt)   1

2 the joule
   the kilowatt hour   2

3 (a) transmission at high voltage allows a lower current
       the lower current reduces the energy loss   2
   (b) so the voltage at home is safer   1

4 *any three: eg.*
   a television
   where electrical energy is transferred to light, sound and heat   3

5 (a)   6

18 p	25.5 p	33 p
0.28 p	0.26 p	0.25 p

   (b) 6-slice toaster (3 kW)
       because it has the highest power rating   2
   (c) 6-slice toaster (3 kW)
       because it toasts most slices at the same time   2
   (d) it toasts enough for more than one customer at a time   1
   (e) if the toaster needs to warm up it could waste energy   1

6 using a high voltage allows a lower current
   so less energy is wasted   2

Examination question

(a) 7 kWh, 4 kWh, 1 kWh, 80.5 kWh
    (only three right gets 1 mark)   2
(b) toaster   1
(c) the kettle has twice the power
    the kettle is used for twice as much time
    $2 \times 2 \times 8 = 32$ p   3

Examiner's Tip ✓

Remember that power is sometimes given in watts. To change
watts to kilowatts you need to divide the number by 1000.

Multiple choice questions

1	1 or 2 = A or D, 3 or 4 = B or C	4	6	(a) A		1
2	C	1		(b) C		1
3	C	1	7	(a) D		1
4	D	1		(b) C		1
5	B	1	8	B		1

TOPIC 5 – Generating electricity   (pages 26–27)
Homework questions

1 *any three from:* hydroelectric, geothermal, wave, wind, solar   3
2 *any three from:* coal, gas, oil, nuclear power   3
3 (a) show energy transfer from light to electrical   1
   (b) show energy transfer:
       from nuclear to thermal
       from thermal to kinetic
       from kinetic to electrical   3

4 steam is produced (naturally)
   the heat source is hot rocks deep underground
   the steam is used to turn a turbine
   the turbine turns the generator   4

5 *two advantages from:*
   does not produce atmospheric pollution, adequate fuel supplies,
   comparatively small amount of fuel needed   2
   two disadvantages from:
   produces nuclear waste, expensive to decommission, possibility
   of a nuclear accident, possible terrorist target   2

6 (a) electricity demand varies
       need a reserve available when there are surges in demand   2
   (b) gas-fired power stations have a short start-up time   1

7 (a) *reasons in favour (either scheme):*
       uses a renewable resource,
       there is no atmospheric pollution   2
   (b) *reasons against:*
       Tidal: loss of natural habitat (eg. mud flats), loss of amenity
       (eg. can't use the beach)
       Wind: noise pollution, may spoil natural beauty of the area   2
   (c) generators that use wave energy   1

8 (a) *two from:*
       introduction of nuclear energy; development of renewable
       methods; increased use of gas and oil   2
   (b) *two from:*
       more control of carbon emissions; more control of sulfur
       emissions; more concern about global warming   2

Examination question

(a) gas   1
(b) fuel-burning power stations can produce electricity all of
    the time   1
    wind generators can only produce electricity when the wind
    is blowing   1
(c) no fuel is burnt   1

Examiner's Tip ✓

Renewable methods of generating electricity usually cause less
pollution than non-renewable methods.

Multiple choice questions

1	1C, 2A, 3B, 4D	4		6	A		1
2	B	1		7	C		1
3	C	1		8	D		1
4	D	1		9	B		1
5	D	1		10	(a) C		1
					(b) D		1

TOPIC 6 – The electromagnetic spectrum
Homework questions   (pages 32–33)

1 hertz (or kilohertz or megahertz)   1

2 it reduces the amount of UV absorbed by the skin   1
   ultra-violet radiation can cause sunburn or skin cancer   1

3 (a) gamma rays ... 1
(b) infra-red wave ... 1
(c) gamma – no refraction, little absorption, no reflection ... 1
light – refracted and absorbed (less strongly), some is reflected ... 1
infra-red – refracted and absorbed, some is reflected ... 1

4 (a) it absorbs the energy from the microwaves ... 1
(b) because water in the food strongly absorbs the microwave energy ... 1
(c) so that the electromagnetic radiation cannot injure people ... 1

5 microwaves can pass through the atmosphere
but radio waves are reflected or absorbed ... 1 1

6 radio wave frequency is about a million times higher because the speed is faster, and frequency = speed ÷ wavelength ... 2

7 (a) wave speed = frequency × wavelength
$300\,000\,000 = 226\,000\,000 \times$ wavelength
wavelength $= 300\,000\,000 \div 226\,000\,000$
$= 1.33$ m ... 3
(b) analogue signals are continuously varying ... 1
digital signals are only on and off ... 1
(c) the digital pulses can be regenerated ... 1

Examination question

Microwaves – to communicate via satellites ... 1
Infra-red rays – to change TV channels ... 1
Ultra-violet rays – to see security markings ... 1
X-rays – to take shadow pictures of bones ... 1
Gamma rays – to sterilise surgical instruments ... 1

Examiner's Tip ✓
Make sure you learn the uses of the different parts of the electromagnetic spectrum.

Multiple choice questions

1	1C, 2A, 3B, 4D	4		6		**B**	1
2	**A**	1		7	(a)	**A**	1
3	**D**	1			(b)	**B**	1
4	**D**	1		8		**A**	1
5	**B**	1		9		**C**	1
				10		**A**	1

TOPIC 7 – Radioactivity   (pages 36–37)
Homework questions

1 counts per second (or the bequerel) ... 1

2 alpha particle   beta particle   gamma ray ... 3

3 (a) measure the count rate from a source of gamma rays
put the cloth in between the source and the detector
measure the count again to see if there is any reduction ... 3
(b) gamma rays pass through most materials ... 1

4 (a) alpha particles have a positive charge
made of 2 protons and 2 neutrons (or a helium nucleus) ... 2
(b) alpha particles are absorbed by a few centimetres of air
so very few are likely to reach her ... 2
(c) if she breathes in the gas, alpha particles will be emitted inside her lungs
all of the alpha particles are likely to be absorbed in her body ... 2
(d) the **time** taken for
half of the radioactive nuclei in a sample to decay ... 2

5 (a) dependent variable = count rate ... 1

(b)
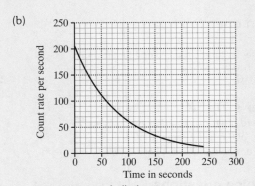

axes correct and all plotting ... 3
(c) time for count rate to halve is 56 seconds ... 1
so half-life of the sample is 56 seconds ... 1
(d) radiation from some other source was being counted ... 1
eg. background radiation ... 1

Examination question

Using the card greatly reduces the count rate because the card absorbs alpha particles ... 1
Using the metal further reduces the count rate because the metal absorbs beta particles ... 1
We know that there is no gamma radiation present because once the alpha particles and beta particles are removed the count is so low that it indicates only background radiation is present ... 1

Examiner's Tip ✓
In order to get marks you need to explain carefully the significance of the decrease in the values given in the table.

Multiple choice questions

1	1D, 2 or 3 = B or C, 4A	4		6	(a)	**D**	1
2	**A**	1			(b)	**C**	1
3	**D**	1		7		**D**	1
4	**C**	1		8		**C**	1
5	**A**	1		9		**A**	1
				10		**A**	1

TOPIC 8 – The origins of the Universe
Homework questions   (pages 40–41)

1 the big bang theory ... 1
2 the red-shift ... 1
3 the further away the galaxy
the larger the red-shift in the light we receive from it ... 2
4 advantages, any *two* from:
clearer images; no atmospheric distortion; can observe ultra-violet and infra-red radiation (that would be absorbed by the atmosphere) ... 2
disadvantages, any *two* from:
launch costs; difficult to repair; needs to be automatic ... 2
5 (a) the wavelength is longer ... 1
(b) the frequency is lower ... 1
6 (a) the galaxy is moving away ... 1
(b) the radio waves and the X-rays will also have a red-shift ... 1
7 if galaxies were getting closer, the wavelength would be shortened ... 1
blue-shift or violet-shift ... 1
8 (a) *two ideas from:*
observations appear to fit the theory
the observations have been made by independent scientists
the observations have been made with different types of radiation ... 2
(b) by repeating results
by designing the investigation well ... 2

Examination answers and tips

Examination question

(a) the Universe started from one point that exploded   1
and created space and matter   1

(b) (i) the wavelength of radiation from galaxies is moved towards
the red end of the spectrum   1

   (ii) red-shift means that galaxies are moving away   1
the bigger the red-shift, the faster they are moving   1
the bigger the red-shift, the further away they are   1
so we think the Universe is expanding   1

Examiner's Tip ✓

*If the galaxies are moving away from us then the distance is
increasing. If the distances are increasing then the Universe is
getting bigger.*

Multiple choice questions

1	1D, 2C, 3B, 4A	4	7	B	1
2	D	1	8	C	1
3	A	1	9	A	1
4	B	1	10	D	1
5	C	1	11	B	1
6	A	1			

TOPIC 9 – Velocity and acceleration

Homework questions   (pages 46–47)

1 velocity – m/s   1
acceleration – m/s^2 1

2 both are (distance ÷ time) – so they have the same unit   1
but velocity also has a direction (it is a vector)   1

3 (a)

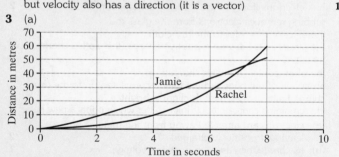

axes correct and all plotting   2
(b) time   1
(c) Rachel won   1
in 7.4 s   1
(d) 47 m   1

4 (a)

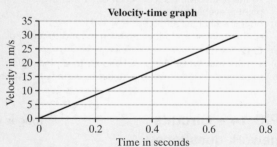

straight line, from origin to (0.7, 30)   2
(b) slope = 30 m/s ÷ 0.7 s   1
acceleration = 43 m/s^2 1
(c) distance = area under the graph
   $= \frac{1}{2} \times 0.7 \times 30$ 1
   = 10.5 m   1
(d) he continues upwards but gravity is slowing him down
eventually he begins to fall   2

Examination questions

1 (a) 3 km   1
   (b) 6.6 minutes (or 6 minutes 36 seconds)   1

2 (a) Quality of written communication   1
Between A and B the car is moving at constant speed.
Between B and C the car moves at a higher constant speed.
Between C and D the car is moving at the same speed as
between A and B.   2
(b) speed = slope of graph   1
slope = (350 − 100) ÷ (7 − 3) = 250 ÷ 4   1
speed = 62.5 m/s   1

TOPIC 10 – Forces   (pages 50–51)

Homework questions

1 the newton   1

2 weight = mass × gravitational field strength
   = 25 × 10 = 250 N   1

3 (a) his weight and the air resistance are equal and opposite
forces, the resultant force is zero   2
(b) your graph should look like the graph on page 49   1
(c) increased air resistance slows him
until the forces are equal again   2

4 (a)

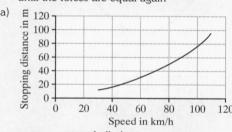

axes correct and all plotting   3
(b) stopping distance   1
(c) the faster the speed, the longer the stopping distance   1
(d) about 40 m   1
(e) by repeating measurements   1
(f) mass of the car, brakes, tyres
surface conditions (wet, icy, or if there is a slope)
driver's reaction time   3

5 (a) acceleration = force ÷ mass = 27 000 ÷ 100 000
   = 0.27 m/s^2 2
(b) force = mass × acceleration = 60 × 0.27
   =16.2 N   2
(c) the same size (16.2 N)   1

Examination question

(a) force **X** = weight   1
force **Y** = viscous drag (friction force)   1
(b) (i) between **A** and **B** the speed is increasing   1
because force **X** is bigger than force **Y**   1
(ii) the speed between **C** and **D** is constant   1
because as the ball moves faster through the oil the
friction force (force **Y**) increases   1
while force **X** stays the same   1
eventually, force **Y** equals force **X** so the speed is
constant   1

TOPIC 11 – Work and energy   (pages 54–55)

Homework questions

1 the joule   1
2 kinetic energy is transferred to heat and sound   3
3 kinetic energy depends on mass, the bus has more mass   1
4 (a) work done = force × distance = 1200 × 2
   = 2400 J   2

(b) it is gravitational potential energy of the weight 1
(c) it transfers to kinetic energy and then to heat and sound ... 1

5 distance = work done ÷ force = 1250 ÷ 500
= 2.5 m 2

6 force = work done ÷ distance = 800 ÷ 20
= 40 N 2

7 (a) work done = force × distance = 110 × 0.5
= 55 J 2
(b) some energy is wasted, eg. as heat in the bow 1
(c) kinetic energy = $\frac{1}{2}mv^2$,
so the arrow velocity = $\sqrt{(2 \times 27 \div 0.02)}$
= 52 m/s 2

Examination questions

1

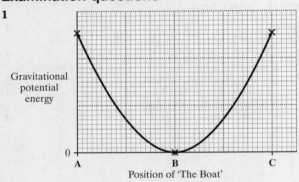

Gravitational
potential
energy

0

A   B   C

Position of 'The Boat' 3

2 (a) (i) work done = force × distance moved (in
the direction of the force) 1
(ii) work done = (700 N + 500 N) × 200 m 1
work done = 1200 N × 200 m
work done = 240 000 J 2
(b) power = work done ÷ time taken
= 240 000 J ÷ (5 × 60) s 1
= 240 000 J ÷ 300 s = 800 W 1
(c) (i) the power output needs to be larger because more than
one chair is being lifted and the chairs have weight ... 1
(ii) electrical, potential 1

TOPIC 12 – Momentum   (pages 58–59)
Homework questions

1 kilogram metre/second (kg m/s) 1

2 momentum has both size and direction
vector quantities have a direction 2

3 (a) in a crash, the crumple zone takes time to squash, reducing
the force 1
(b) an air bag changes momentum over a longer time, reducing
the force 1
(c) a seat belt stretches in a crash, taking longer to slow the
person 1

4 the car's speed has not changed, but its velocity has
momentum depends on velocity, so momentum has changed too
a force is needed to change momentum 3

5 (material flies off in all directions) the momentum in any direction
is balanced by the momentum in the opposite direction 2

6 (a) momentum before = (20 × 2.5) + (20 × 0)
= 50 kg m/s
momentum after = (20 × 0) + (20 × 2)
= 40 kg m/s 4
(b) energy has been lost (eg. as sound) 1
(c) when they were touching, there was a force on
each of the stones 1
(d) force = change of momentum ÷ time
= 64 ÷ 0.8
= 80 N 2

Examination question

(a) (i) momentum = mass × velocity 1
(ii) momentum = 0.75 kg × 15.0 m/s 1
momentum = 11.25 kg m/s 1
the direction is downwards 1

Examiner's Tip ✓
An alternative unit for momentum is the newton second (Ns).

(iii) change in momentum = 11.25 kg m/s 1
(iv) force = change in momentum ÷ time taken 1
(v) force = 11.25 N ÷ 0.1 s 1
force = 112.5 N 2
(b) in a car crash the person wearing a seat belt will undergo a large
change in momentum 1
the seat belt increases the time taken for this change to occur ... 1
this reduces the force on the person 1
this reduces the chance of serious injury 1

TOPIC 13 – Static electricity   (pages 64–65)
Homework questions

1 a repulsion 1

2 also a repulsion 1

3 rate of flow of charge = electric current 1

4 lightning strike (and possible electrocution)
sparks can cause fires 2

5 (a) he could have been charged by friction
electrons could have been transferred by rubbing 2
(b) excess charge can flow through the cable
electrons flow in the cable to discharge him 2

6 rubbing removes electrons from the glass rod
the electrons transfer to the dry cloth
the glass rod is left with a positive charge (the cloth's charge is
negative) 3

7 the photocopier 'drum' is charged up
an image of the page to be copied is projected on to the drum
charge leaks away where the light is brighter
the remaining charge attracts ink powder which prints a new page ... 4

8 (a) electrons are attracted away from the metal sphere
leaving it positively charged 2
(b) as charge increases, so does the voltage 1
(c) if the voltage is big enough, a spark can jump through the air ... 1

Examination questions

1 (a) similar charges repel
so the paint droplets repel each other and the
paint is evenly spread 1
(b) opposite charges attract
so the paint sticks to the car, even in hard-to-reach places ... 1

2 (a) C B E A D 3
(b) a spark may cause the petrol vapour to explode 1
to prevent this, connect the tanker to earth with a wire 1

TOPIC 14 – Circuits   (pages 68–69)
Homework questions

1 the ohm (Ω) 1

2

⊏▭⊐ fuse 1

⊏▭⊐ resistor 1

⊏▱⊐ thermistor 1

3 (a) $4\frac{1}{2}$ V $(= 3 \times 1\frac{1}{2}$ V) 1
(b) the voltage would be $1\frac{1}{2}$ V $(= 1\frac{1}{2}$ V $+ 1\frac{1}{2}$ V $- 1\frac{1}{2}$ V)
his torch would light dimly or not at all 2

4 for current in one direction, the diode has a fairly low resistance;
for current in the reverse direction, the resistance is very high .. 2

5 the resistance of the LDR becomes lower in brighter light; the
current in the circuit increases; the lamp gets a bit brighter 3

6 (a)

[Graph: Resistance (y-axis, 0 to 12) vs Voltage (x-axis, 0 to 20), showing an increasing curve]

axes correct and all points plotted 3
(b) the lamp filament became hotter 1
(c) when the p.d. is 12 V, the resistance = 10.3 Ω (from the
table or the graph)
current = potential difference ÷ resistance
    $= 12 ÷ 10.3 = 1.17$ A 2

7 (a) resistance = voltage ÷ current 1
    $= 1$ V $÷ 0.002$ A $= 500$ Ω 1
(b) 0.002 A (components in series have the same current) .. 1
(c) (i) it decreases, because component **A** is a thermistor .. 1
    (ii) it increases, because the total circuit resistance is less .. 1
    (iii) it increases, because component **B** has a bigger share
        of the 2 V 1

Examination questions

1 **C** is the graph for the 3-volt filament lamp 1
    because the resistance increases 1
    as the lamp gets hotter 1

> **Examiner's Tip** ✓
> *Make sure you know the shapes of the current–p.d. graphs for a
> resistor, a filament lamp and a diode.*

2 (a) (i) potential difference = current × resistance 1
    (ii) $V = 230 ÷ 20 = 11.5$ V
        $R = V ÷ I$
        $R = 11.5$ V $÷ 0.25$ A
        $R = 46$ Ω 4
    (iii) total resistance = $46 × 20 = 920$ Ω 1
(b) as the temperature increases, the resistance increases .. 1

TOPIC 15 – Mains electricity   (pages 72–73)
Homework questions

1 live, neutral, earth 3

2 *any three* of: earth wire, fuse, cable grip, plastic top, plastic
insulation on pins for live and neutral 3

3 your diagram should look like the one on page 70, with the
same colours and labels 3

4 'direct current' is a flow of charge
it always passes in the same direction 2

5 a large current heats up the thin wire in the fuse
the fuse wire melts and this breaks the circuit 2

6 if a fault connects the case to the live wire
then a large current flows to earth and melts the fuse
the large current stops before it can cause a dangerous fire .. 3

7 (a) 230 V
    alternating current (a.c.) 2
(b) (close to) zero 1

8 (a) alternating current (a.c.) 1
(b) he should use the brightness (intensity) control
    and the x-shift (↔) control 2
(c) +5 V 1
(d) 10 V (between −5 V and +5 V) 1
(e) 1 cycle takes 0.02 second
    frequency = 1 ÷ 0.02 = 50 Hz 3
(f) focus the trace to make it as clear as possible
    choose the most appropriate time-base (sweep speed)
    setting for the frequency he is measuring 2

Examination questions

1 (a) cable contains 3 wires each covered with a different colour
    of plastic insulation
    these wires are enclosed in an outer layer of insulating plastic
    the cable is flexible 3
(b) connect brown wire to live terminal
    connect blue wire to neutral terminal
    connect green/yellow wire to earth terminal 1
    strip the insulation from the ends of the wires and
    use the screws to connect the wires firmly to the terminals .. 1

2 (a) the kettle is made of metal, which conducts,
    the hair-dryer is made of plastic, which does not 1
(b) if the metal case of the kettle became live 1
    anyone touching the case could be electrocuted 1
    the earth wire connects the case to earth 1
    so current will flow through the wire rather than anyone
    touching the case 1

TOPIC 16 – Power in electrical appliances
Homework questions   (pages 76–77)

1 the watt (W) 1

2 'electric current' is a flow
of electric charge 2

3 power = current × potential difference = 0.4 × 230 = 92 W .. 2

4 (a) if current flows in a resistor, electrical energy is transferred
    to heat 1
(b) energy transferred = power × time = 1200 × 60
    = 72 000 J 2
(c) current = power ÷ p.d. = 1200 ÷ 230
    = 5.2 A 2
(d) fuse rating must be more than 5.2 A, the next common
    size is 13 A 1

5 (a) energy = power × time = current × p.d. × time
    = 0.25 × 2.2 × 1
    = 0.55 J 2
(b) the p.d. is lower
    so each coulomb of charge transfers less energy 2

6 (a) current = power ÷ p.d. = 10 W ÷ 230 V
    = 0.043 A 2
(b) energy transferred = p.d. × charge = 230 V × 1 C
    = 230 J 2
(c) charge = current × time = 10 W ÷ 230 V × 3600 s
    = 157 C 2

Examination questions

1 (a) 800 W 1
(b) (i) power = current × voltage 1
    (ii) current = power ÷ voltage = 800 W ÷ 230 V 1
        = 3.5 (amperes, A) 1
    (iii) 5 A 1

2 (a) positively charged 1
because they are attracted towards the negative spoon and
opposite charges attract (*see* topic 13) 1
(b) (i) charge = current × time 1
(ii) charge = 0.5 A × (30 × 60) s 1
charge = 900 C 1

TOPIC 17 – Radioactive decay; Fission and fusion (pages 80–81)

Homework questions

1 ions 1

2 (a) *Masses:* electron = very small (negligible)
proton = 1 unit
neutron = 1 unit 3
(b) *Charges:* electron = −1 unit (negative)
proton = +1 unit (positive)
neutron = no charge (neutral) 3

3 fission happens when a nucleus splits into smaller particles
energy is usually released 2

4 uranium-235 or plutonium-239 1

5 the nucleus (*eg.* uranium-235) is hit by a neutron and splits
into:
two daughter nuclei
and two or three more neutrons
some of these neutrons hit other uranium-235 nuclei
and the process continues 5

6 *any two advantages from:*
does not produce atmospheric pollution; adequate fuel supplies;
comparatively small amount of fuel needed 2

any two disadvantages from:
produces nuclear waste; expensive to decommission; possibility
of a nuclear accident; possible terrorist target 2

7 (a) atoms of the same element can have different numbers of
neutrons
these different versions of the same element are called
'isotopes' 2
(b) number of protons in the nucleus is reduced by 2
number of neutrons in the nucleus is reduced by 2 2

8 the joining together of 2 small atomic nuclei to form a larger
one 2

9 (a) most alpha particles went straight on
some alpha particles were deflected
a few alpha particles bounced back 3
(b) because so many alpha particles missed, the
nucleus must be small
because it repelled alpha particles, the nucleus
must be positive too 2
(c) other scientists confirmed their results with independent
studies 1

Examination questions

1 (a)

Neutron
Proton
Electron
3
(b) neutron 1
7 1
(c) this is the total number of protons and neutrons
in the nucleus 1

2 (a) **Y** and **Z** 1
they have the same number of protons 1

(b) quality of written communication 1
Path A: The alpha particle passes straight through the empty
space of the atom
Path B: The positively-charged alpha particle is deflected by
the positively-charged nucleus
Path C: The alpha particle is heading straight for
the nucleus and is repelled backwards 2

Examiner's Tip ✓
*You would get 2 marks for correctly explaining 3 tracks, or 1
mark for correctly explaining 2 or 1 tracks.*

Topic 18 – Turning effect of moments; Moving in a circle (pages 86–87)

Homework questions

1 the turning effect of a force 1

2 moment = 8 N × 0.7 m = 5.6 N m 2

3 (a) move closer to the middle to reduce the moment 2
(b) no effect because the moments are balanced 2

4 (a) centre of mass 1
(b) by repeating the measurement eg. hanging the
card from a different position 1

5 (a) centripetal force increases because the speed is greater 2
(b) the centre of mass of the tall car is higher so there is a larger
moment making the car roll over 2
(c) the radius has decreased so the centripetal force needed is
greater 2
(d) for safety the car can be designed to be less
likely to roll over 2

Examination questions

1 change in velocity or direction (or an acceleration) 1
needs a force towards the centre 1
provided by friction 1

2 (a) (i) a plumbline (or a description of one) 1
(ii) *any 4 from:*
Hang card from one hole with a pin.
Hang a plumbline from the pin.
Draw (a vertical) along the plumbline.
Repeat using the other hole.
The centre of mass is where the two lines cross. 4
(b) at the intersection of the diagonals of the rectangle 1
at the centre of the circle 1
one third of the way along a median (line joining a corner
to the mid-point of opposite side) 1

TOPIC 19 – Planets and satellites (pages 90–91)

Homework questions

1 24 hours or 1 day 1

2 Saturn 1

3 the satellite can monitor the ground in strips as the Earth turns
a low satellite orbits quickly so it monitors the next strip sooner 2

4 (a) gravitational forces attract masses 1
(b) apple and orange because they both have more mass than
the grape 2

5 (a) it takes longer to go around the Earth
because it has moved further from the Earth 2
(b) the space shuttle moves to a lower orbit
will orbit closer to the Earth at a higher speed 2

6 (a) the gravitational attraction between the Sun and Mercury   2
   (b) the orbits of planets are slightly squashed circles (ellipses) so
     the radius varies   2
   (c) circumference = $2 \times \pi \times$ (58 million km)
     = 364 million km
     speed = distance ÷ time
     speed = 364 million km ÷ 88 days
       = 4.1 million km/day (or 48 km/s)   3

Examination question

(a) (i) satellites stay in orbit because of their high speed and the
      force of gravity between the satellite and the Earth   2
   (ii) the time will be longer   1
(b) (i) geostationary   1
   (ii) a geostationary satellite is always over the same point on
      the Earth   1
(c) (i) low polar orbit   1
   (ii) as the Earth spins beneath them, the satellites can scan
      different areas of the Earth   1

TOPIC 20 – Mirrors and Lenses   (pages 94–95)
Homework questions

1 *Similarity:* either virtual or upright   1
   Difference: images in convex mirrors are smaller
   (but are the same size in plane mirrors)   1
2 rays from the Sun should be drawn parallel
   the reflected rays should all pass through the focus
   the distance between the mirror and the focus is the focal length
   (see diagram on page 92)   3
3 refraction   1
4 *Labels on:* the incident ray, the reflected ray, the normal   3
   the angle of incidence and the angle of reflection should be
   equal (see diagram on page 92)   1
5 (a) a convex (converging) lens   1
   (b) real, inverted and smaller ('diminished')   1
   (c) rays from the object are refracted to meet at the image
     the ray that goes through the centre of the lens goes
     straight on
     a real, inverted, smaller (diminished) image is formed where
     the rays cross   3
   (d) magnification = image height ÷ object height
     = 0.008 m ÷ 8 m
     = 0.001 or 1/1000 (no unit)   3
   (e) magnification is a ratio of two heights   1
   (f) object distance is less
     but the image distance is about the same
     so the magnification is more than it was (but it's still a
     small image)   3
6 reflecting telescopes have a mirror to reflect the light
   refracting telescopes have a lens to refract the light   2

Examination question

(a) (i) where the rays cross   1
   (ii) a converging lens   1
(b) (i)

                         1
   (ii) a diverging lens   1
(c) converging   **1**   smaller than   1
   film   **1**   nearer to   1
(d) (i) the image is bigger than the object   1
   (ii) a real image is one where the rays of light cross and can
      form an image on a screen   1

Examiner's Tip ✓
Make sure you know the difference between a real image and a virtual image.

TOPIC 21 – Sound; Ultrasound   (pages 98–99)
Homework questions

1 hertz (or kilohertz)   1
2 the higher the frequency, the higher the pitch of the sound   1
3 the quality depends on the type of waveform
   different waveforms sound different even if the pitch is the
   same   2
4 *any three similarities from:* a longitudinal wave; mechanical
   vibrations; cannot pass through a vacuum; can be
   reflected/refracted   3
   any one difference from: sound frequencies are
   between 20 Hz and 20 000 Hz; ultrasound frequencies are
   above 20 000 Hz; ultrasound can be used for scanning and
   cleaning   1
5 (a) sound 2 has a higher frequency
     both sounds have the same amplitude   2
   (b) the waveform is different
     so the sounds have a different quality   2
   (c) there are three cycles in four squares
     which is three vibrations in $4 \times 0.000\ 025$ second
     so the frequency = 3 ÷ 0.0001 s = 30 000 Hz
     this is ultrasound, which she cannot hear   4
6 speed = distance ÷ time or 1500 m/s = d ÷ 0.0001 s
   d = 0.15 m (15 cm)
   but the ultrasound travelled there and back
   so the depth 15 ÷ 2 = 7.5 cm   4

Examination questions

1 (a) vibrates   1
   (b) (i) higher   1
      (ii) louder   1
   (c) (i) ultrasound   1
      (ii) they are at a higher frequency (pitch)
        than can be heard by the human ear   2
2 the ultrasonic waves shake the dirt loose
   without having to take the watch to pieces   2

TOPIC 22 – Movement from electricity
Homework questions   (pages 102–103)

1 *any three from:* vacuum cleaner; DVD player; washing machine;
   electric fan; central heating water pump, etc.   3
2 (a) from left to right (N to S)   1
   (b) the forces reverse
     and the motor spins the other way   2
   (c) no change (reversing the current cancels out the effect of
     reversing the magnetic field)   1
   (d) for both forces the magnetic field is in the **same** direction,
     but the current for each is in the **opposite** direction   2
   (e) increasing the current (or the number of turns
     on the coil), increasing the magnetic field   2
3 (a) it moves to the right   1
   (b) it moves to and fro   1
   (c) the coil moves with more force   1
   (d) the coil moves with more force   1

Examination questions

1 (a) reverse the direction of the current   1
     reverse the direction of the magnetic field   1

(b) increase the current, or the magnetic field ... 1
increase the number of turns of wire on the coil ... 1

2 (a) the force ... 1

(b)

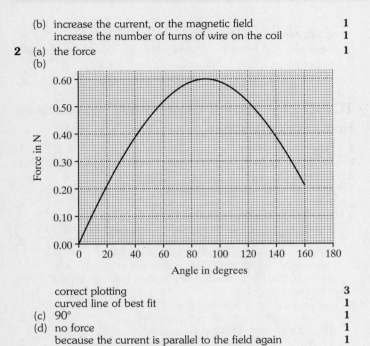

correct plotting ... 3
curved line of best fit ... 1

(c) 90° ... 1

(d) no force ... 1
because the current is parallel to the field again ... 1

TOPIC 23 – Electromagnetic induction, Generators; Transformers (pages 106–107)

Homework questions

1 primary coil, secondary coil, soft iron core ... 3

2 step-down ... 1

3 (a) a.c. current (the magnet moves first one way and then the other and so does the current) ... 1

(b) (i) increases the potential difference ... 1
(ii) decreases the potential difference ... 1
(iii) increases the potential difference ... 1
(iv) decreases the potential difference ... 1

4 the current from the battery is d.c., the transformer needs a.c. in the primary coil for it to work ... 2

5 the slip rings and brushes complete the circuit but allow the coil to turn ... 2

6 number of turns on secondary = number of turns on primary × p.d. across secondary ÷ p.d. across primary = 4600 × 12 V ÷ 230 V = 240 turns ... 2

Examination questions

1 rotate the coil faster ... 1
twice as fast ... 1

2 (a) (i) transformer **A** increases (steps-up) the voltage ... 1
before transmission via the National Grid ... 1
(ii) transformer **B** steps down the voltage ... 1
to make it safer for domestic use ... 1

(b) transmission at a high voltage allows a low current ... 1
energy is lost from the cable as heat ... 1
the lower the current the lower the energy loss ... 1

(c) an alternating voltage across the primary coil creates a changing magnetic field which induces an alternating voltage in the secondary coil ... 1
a direct voltage across the primary coil creates a magnetic field which is not changing so no voltage is induced in the secondary coil ... 1

TOPIC 24 – The Life of a Star (pages 110–111)

Homework questions

1 The Milky Way ... 1

2 star *(smallest)*, galaxy, Universe *(biggest)* ... 1

3 gravitational forces pull inwards
pressure from radiation presses outwards ... 2

4 dust and gas (a nebula) are attracted by gravity
they are gradually pulled together to form a denser mass
when a fusion reaction starts, the star begins to radiate
some of the material may form planets ... 4

5 stars have huge amounts of hydrogen
there is enough fuel for millions of years of fusion ... 2

6 stars with a smaller mass start as a yellow dwarf
eventually the star expands to form a red giant
then gravity takes over and the star collapses to form a white dwarf
eventually the star runs out of fuel, forms a black dwarf ... 4

7 (a) our Sun is a yellow dwarf star
the next stage is to become a red giant ... 2
(b) our Sun does not have enough mass to form a red supergiant so it will not explode as it contracts ... 2

8 (a) a neutron star or a black hole ... 2
(b) a neutron star is a very dense dwarf star
but a black hole is so dense that the pull of gravity stops anything (even light) escaping from it ... 2

9 (a) heavier elements formed from hydrogen by fusion
lighter nuclei join together to form heavier ones ... 2
(b) when a star explodes (supernova) ... 1

Examination questions

1 (a) **D A C B** ... 3
(b) **A** ... 1

2 (a) The Sun is subject to two balanced forces:
The force making it contract is gravity.
The force making it expand is due to the pressure from fusion. ... 3

(b) (i) *any three points from:* hydrogen is used up; the star will expand; and become a red giant; it will contract under gravity; to become a white dwarf ... 3
(ii) *any three points from:* it may explode; and become a supernova; throwing dust and gas into space; leaving a dense neutron star (or a black hole) ... 3

3 (a) *any two points from:*
the nuclei of light elements fuse together;
each fusion reaction releases energy (or light or heat);
there are lots of reactions ... 2
(b) the Sun contains heavy elements as well as hydrogen ... 1

Examiner's Tip ✓

Make sure that you know the difference between fusion (when nuclei join together) and fission (when a nucleus breaks apart).